SELF-DEVELOPMENT FOR MANAGERS
A major new series of workbooks for managers edited by Jane Cranwell-Ward

This series presents a selection of books in workbook format, on a range of key management issues and skills. The books are designed to provide practising managers with the basis for self-development across a wide range of industries and occupations.

Each book relates to other books in the series to provide a coherent new approach to self-development for managers. Closely based on the latest management training initiatives, the books are designed to complement management development programmes, in-house company training, and management qualification programmes such as CMS, DMS, MBA and professional qualification programmes.

Other books in the series:

Thriving on Stress
Jane Cranwell-Ward

Managing Change
Colin Carnall

Effective Problem Solving
Dave Francis

The series editor **Jane Cranwell-Ward** is the Director of Company Programmes at Henley – The Management College. She is the author of *Managing Stress* (Pan, 1986).

Developing Assertiveness

Anni Townend

ROUTLEDGE

First published 1991
by Routledge
11 New Fetter Lane, London EC4P 4EE

Printed in Great Britain by Biddles Ltd,
Guildford and King's Lynn

British Library Cataloguing in Publication Data

Townend, Anni
    Developing Assertiveness – (Self-Development for
    Managers).
    1. Managers. Assertive behaviour – Manuals
    I. Title   II. Series
    658.4094

ISBN 0–415–04464–2

Contents

Preface

Faced with the challenges of the twenty-first century all managers must develop the range of competencies needed to be effective. The series Self Development for Managers has been created to help managers equip themselves. The topics have been selected in such a way that each book complements one another.

Managers frequently report spending up to 80 per cent of their time communicating with people. Therefore, a core competency for managers is the ability to develop positive relationships with others, including superiors, peers and subordinates. Particularly in times of change managers can feel threatened and defensive, thus adopting a passive, manipulative or aggressive approach to people. Behaving assertively towards others will ensure effective relationships.

In the 1970s when books were first being written on assertiveness, the bias was towards women becoming more assertive. Gradually the emphasis has shifted, and today as many men as women recognise the importance of building assertiveness.

Developing Assertiveness has been written in a step-by-step format drawing on the theory of Transactional Analysis. First, managers can identify the stances they take in relation to others – passive, manipulative, aggressive or assertive. The reader is then offered a range of proven techniques for developing assertiveness. The workbook approach, characteristic of the series, helps the reader take positive steps to change attitudes and behaviour when necessary to become more assertive. The final section of the workbook helps the reader develop and maintain assertiveness in others. Once more the reader is given techniques to use.

Anni Townend has several years of experience training managers to develop assertiveness. She is a regular contributor on management development programmes at Henley and also works as an independent consultant. Many of the techniques described in the book have been used successfully by managers. Her creative approach has made her a valuable contributor to the series.

Jane Cranwell-Ward
Series Editor

Introduction

Developing Assertiveness is written for you, the practising manager. The book will help you to not only develop assertiveness in yourself and others but also to maintain assertiveness in yourself, your relationship with others and in others. The term 'manager' is used in its broadest sense to include anyone who is responsible for managing other people. Thus a manager may be someone who is responsible for managing an individual and/or a team of people at any level of the organization.

Assertiveness is about having confidence in yourself, a positive attitude about yourself and towards others, and it is about behaving towards others in a way which is direct and honest. Thus developing assertiveness in yourself is about having a positive attitude about yourself and towards others as well as behaving towards others in a way which is open. Assertiveness is not about getting what you want at the expense of others but is often about not getting what you want in the sense that the more assertive you are the more assertive others will be with you. This means that they will assert themselves too!

The advantage of developing assertiveness in yourself and others is that between you you will develop working relationships which are about trust. Most importantly, you will know where you stand with one another as well as helping one another to be positive.

My own interest in the subject of assertiveness began many years ago when I realized that I lacked self-confidence. Indeed my image of myself was negative and I had a tendency to focus on the negative in myself and others. Fortunately, I was encouraged by friends and colleagues to develop a positive and affirmative view of myself which led me to work with others who lacked self-confidence and wanted to develop assertiveness. Initially I worked primarily with women who, like myself, recognized that they needed to develop their self-confidence and an image of themselves which was positive and affirmative of themselves as women.

However, after a few years of running assertion training courses for women I was invited by several organizations to run training courses for women and men. Whilst these courses tended to be called interpersonal skills training, in essence they too were about helping managers to develop self-confidence, a positive attitude and assertive behaviour.

More recently I have been working with senior managers and managers within organizations running courses in team-building and team-working. Again, underpinning many of the skills required for effective team-working are those of assertiveness, in particular, respect for one another and for each others' differences. One of the reasons many managers lack confidence is that they feel their way of working is neither respected nor understood. The result is that managers become competitive with one another within their working group and/or team and with other teams, or other divisions, in the same organization. A group of individuals who are working together effectively as a team have a positive attitude and behave assertively with one another.

All too often working relationships suffer from not being open and honest simply through a lack of understanding of appropriate communication skills which encourage a positive attitude and assertiveness. Typically people feel that they are not valued, neither for what they do nor for who they are, irrespective of what they do. This sometimes results in them losing interest in and commitment to their work, or in them becoming determined to show others that they can do the job – often without anyone else. Either way these people have difficulty in managing others effectively, and are equally difficult for others to manage.

Many managers with whom I have worked on developing assertiveness in themselves and others, having realized their own underlying lack of self-confidence, have reported how very differently they have felt towards one another as a result of feeling more positive in themselves.

When you have a positive attitude towards yourself and others you experience others as being more positive towards you. On a 'good day' you are more creative and productive, whereas on a so-called 'bad day' nothing seems to go right. Recognizing and understanding your own attitude and behaviour is the beginning of developing assertiveness. Once you are aware of your attitude and behaviour you can begin to look at ways of consciously changing your attitude and choosing your behaviour. All too often we are so used to our negative attitudes and non-assertive behaviours that we are oblivious not only to ourselves but also to the impact of these negative attitudes and non-assertive behaviours on others.

Whether you are a manager looking to develop assertiveness in yourself so that you manage your peers, subordinates and/or boss more effectively, this book will help you to develop your inner resources in terms of your self-confidence which will in turn help you manage the outer resources more creatively and assertively.

I would like to thank all the people with whom I have worked over the years. Through helping them to develop assertiveness I too have been helped in both developing and maintaining a positive attitude towards myself and others, and assertive behaviour. I would also like to thank the people who have helped me in the writing of this book, in particular Eric Priestly who initiated me into the art of writing on a computer; Peter Handley who has supported me during the writing of this book; and Lisa Handley who has helped to look after our daughter, Fern Handley-Townend, during the first year of her life.

I would also like to say a special thank you to Jane Cranwell-Ward, the editor of the series and the inspiration for writing the book. It is she who has encouraged me at times when I lack the confidence to write, to think positive and to keep on writing! Finally I would like to thank the friends and colleagues with whom I have discussed the content of the book and who have contributed their ideas to it through these discussions.

What is assertiveness?

What is assertiveness and why do people, like yourself, want to develop and maintain it in themselves and others? My own experience, and that of the many managers with whom I have worked, suggests that it is primarily about developing self-confidence. Once you have developed confidence in yourself you have an inner resource of positive feelings and thoughts about yourself and others upon which you can draw. All too often people who are lacking in self-confidence fall prey to negative thoughts and feelings about themselves, and others, which causes them to behave non-assertively. When you feel confident in yourself, and have a positive attitude towards yourself and others, you are more likely to respond assertively to people irrespective of their behaviour.

Assertiveness, then, is about self-confidence, which means having a positive attitude towards yourself and others. It means being honest with yourself and others; and it is about respecting yourself and others. When you are self-confident and your behaviour is assertive you are open to others and their views even though they may be different from your own. You are able to express yourself clearly and to communicate with others effectively.

THE MANAGER'S VIEW OF ASSERTIVENESS

Assertiveness is often confused with aggressive behaviour. Many managers consider themselves and some of their colleagues as not needing to develop assertiveness since they are already 'too assertive'. However, once they start to develop a greater awareness

4

of their attitudes and behaviour they realize that in fact, far from being assertive, their behaviour towards others is aggressive.

The same managers often believe that the only way to do business is to be aggressive towards others; they say that it is the only way of getting things done. This often means that they tend to tell people what to do rather than involving them in making decisions and solving problems; they rarely invite others to put their views forward and they are generally not interested in listening to points of view which are different from their own.

Whilst these managers do get things done and get other people to do things, they do so at the expense of respect and commitment. They neither respect their colleagues nor do they have their colleagues' respect. Indeed these managers often report that they feel isolated from the people with whom they work, which makes team-working difficult for them. They are used to people complying with their wishes rather than being committed to them.

One of the key differences between the manager whose behaviour is assertive and the manager whose behaviour is aggressive is the fact that the manager whose behaviour is assertive is respected by others and she or he respects and values them. Rather than getting others to comply with her or his wishes this manager gets commitment from them.

The managers who do consider themselves as needing to develop assertiveness, are often those who recognize that they lack self-confidence. They tend to view their own behaviour, and others who need to develop assertiveness, as passive. They regularly find it difficult to express themselves and end up complying with the wishes of others. Not surprisingly they report working for and/or alongside people whose behaviour towards others is aggressive.

There tends to be a symbiotic relationship between the manager whose behaviour is aggressive and the manager whose behaviour is passive. The aggressive manager needs to be in control and takes on a lot of responsibility, whilst the passive manager allows others to take control of situations and avoids taking on responsibility, since she or he lacks the confidence to do so.

Managers are frequently surprised to realize that a lack of confidence underlies aggressive behaviour just as it underlies passive behaviour. Indeed behaving aggressively towards others is usually a way of covering up this underlying lack of self-confidence.

For the managers who recognize themselves as behaving aggressively the realization that they can still get things done by being assertive is a big leap forward. In other words they can still give direction to others but in a way which is respecting of others and which maintains others' self-confidence. The big leap forward for the managers who recognize themselves as behaving passively is to realize that the person who is aggressive towards them is also lacking in confidence and that by developing their self-confidence and assertiveness they can influence others' behaviour.

Aggressive and passive behaviours are often the two non-assertive behaviours which managers readily recognize in themselves. There is, however, a third kind of non-assertive behaviour which also results from an underlying lack of self-confidence, and that is manipulative behaviour. In some managers the underlying lack of self-confidence is such that the only way in which they relate to others is by being indirect and devious.

These managers not only feel isolated from their colleagues but also feel depressed in themselves. Many managers report having experienced themselves as behaving manipulatively at times when they have been undergoing some kind of transition, either in their personal or professional lives or both. For these managers it is a big leap forward for them to realize that they can develop assertiveness, albeit slowly, by challenging their negative attitudes about themselves and towards others.

Assertiveness is often seen as being 'selfish', that it is about asserting what 'I want'. Indeed some of the criticisms of assertion training have been that it reflects the 'me culture'. Whilst assertiveness is about asserting yourself it is very much about respecting other people and their views. Several years ago assertiveness was seen as something which women needed to develop, not men. Men were seen as already being assertive. Fortunately, in more recent years this view has changed and assertiveness is now seen as being an integral part of managing yourself and others more effectively through developing openness and trust in our working relationships.

I believe that we can all change our attitudes and behaviour from negative and non-assertive to positive and assertive. It is for this reason that I have drawn upon the theory of Transactional Analysis (TA). TA theory is based on the premise that once we are aware of our attitudes and behaviour we can change them to more positive and affirmative attitudes and behaviour. In particular I have drawn upon the TA theory of Life Positions since the four underlying Life Positions correspond with the four kinds of behaviour already referred to as follows:

- *I'm not OK - You're OK*, Passive behaviour
- *I'm not OK - You're not OK*, Manipulative behaviour
- *I'm OK - You're not OK*, Aggressive behaviour
- *I'm OK - You're OK*, Assertive behaviour

The theory of Life Positions is discussed more fully in *Step Two: What does it mean to be passive, manipulative, aggressive and/or assertive?* Before going on to the self-perception questionnaire, a brief summary of assertion theory and assertion training will further clarify what assertiveness is.

ASSERTION THEORY

Assertion theory is based on the assumptions that: everyone has basic human rights which should be respected; and that assertion skills can be developed. The theory of assertion emphasizes the basic rights that we all have and the responsibilities which go with having these rights. Below is a list of rights which I have added to, from my own experience of assertion training, and adapted from 'A bill of assertive rights' by Manuel J. Smith in *When I Say No I Feel Guilty* and from *A Woman in Your Own Right* by Anne Dickson and *Assertion Training* by Colleen Kelley.

1 I have the right to express my thoughts and opinions, even though they may be different from those of others.
2 I have the right to express my feelings and to take responsibility for them.
3 I have the right to say 'Yes' to people.
4 I have the right to change my mind without making excuses.
5 I have the right to make mistakes and to be responsible for them.
6 I have the right to say 'I don't know'.
7 I have the right to say 'I don't understand'.
8 I have the right to ask for what I want.
9 I have the right to say 'No' without feeling guilty.

10 I have the right to be respected by others, and to respect them.
11 I have the right to be listened to and taken seriously.
12 I have the right to be independent.
13 I have the right to be successful.
14 I have the right to choose not to assert myself.

Assertion theory traditionally distinguishes between three kinds of behaviours in any situation, these are seen along a continuum ranging from non-assertive, to assertive to aggressive. The three behaviours are linked to whether a person respects her or his basic rights and those of others, and to whether a person allows others to violate her or his rights or violates other peoples' rights.

Non-assertive behaviour
The person who behaves non-assertively in a situation does not assert her or his basic rights, instead she or he allows others to infringe upon them.

Assertive behaviour
The person who behaves assertively in a situation asserts her or his basic rights. She or he takes responsibility for them whilst recognizing and respecting the other person's basic rights.

Aggressive behaviour
The person who behaves aggressively in a situation asserts her or his basic rights at the expense of the other person's rights. She or he does not respect that the other person has rights.

The important aspect of any basic right is that it carries with it responsibility. Assertion theory differentiates between those rights which are basic human rights and those which are role rights. Role rights are those which a person has and is responsible for as part of her or his role.

It is not my intention to focus on rights in this workbook. I have, however, discussed the limits of particular rights in specific situations with many managers. The discussions have always been lively. Some of the rights may not be rights with which you feel comfortable. However, it is worth re-reading the list of rights and considering which ones you do feel are your rights and responsibilities. You may also like to consider which ones you feel are your rights and responsibilities and whether you recognize others as having the same rights and responsibilities.

ASSERTION TRAINING

Assertion training is traditionally about helping people to understand assertion theory and to practise the skills of assertion. Through understanding and being aware of the different kinds of behaviour people can learn to take responsibility for their choice of behaviour in any situation. This means that a person may decide, for example, to behave non-assertively or aggressively in a situation but to do so with awareness and to take responsibility for this choice.

The skills of assertion

A great deal of assertion training is about helping people to develop the skills of assertion. The focus of the workbook is not on the skills of assertion, instead the focus is on helping you to develop assertiveness through developing your inner resources and some basic communication skills. You may already be familiar with some of the skills of assertion listed and briefly described below. Indeed, if you have ever attended an assertion training course you will probably be familiar with some of the skills.

The skill of 'broken record'
The 'broken record' is, as the term suggests, about repeating what you have said again and again. It is about calmly persisting and repeating what you think and/or feel without being deflected from what is important to you.

The skill of 'fogging'
Fogging refers to the skills of agreeing in principle with someone when she or he criticizes you. Rather than denying criticism, it is about accepting that there may be some truth in it – in principle. You, however, are the judge as to whether or not it is true of you.

The skill of 'negative assertion'
Another skill for dealing with criticism that is true of you is negative assertion. When someone criticizes you, and you know that the criticism is true, you agree with her or him without apologizing.

Since most people anticipate that people will deny criticisms, when you accept and agree with the criticism it encourages an assertive exchange.

The skill of 'negative inquiry'
Again a skill for dealing with criticism, negative inquiry encourages you to actively seek specific criticism from a person whose criticism is vague and/or general.

These are just a few of the more popular skills of assertion. Whilst this workbook does not focus on specific assertion skills you will find that by working through the steps you will be able to deal with most situations assertively, and on the occasions when your behaviour is non-assertive you will be aware either of your choice not to be assertive or what could have been your assertive option. Enjoy the book!

How to use the book

The book is written in the form of a workbook. This means that you are encouraged not only to read about ways of developing assertiveness in yourself and others but also to use the book in order to develop and maintain assertiveness.

You may find that some of the steps towards developing assertiveness in yourself, and in others, are of immediate value whilst others will be of more long-term value. Either way you will benefit most from working your way through the book step by step, and completing the exercises as you go along.

In order to work through the book it is necessary that you have a clear picture of the overall structure. The book is divided into three parts. In Part I you have an opportunity to develop your self-awareness through assessing and understanding your own attitudes and behaviours. In Part II you look at, and practise, ways of developing and maintaining assertiveness in yourself. In Part III you look at ways of developing and maintaining assertiveness in others.

Within these three parts of the book there are eleven steps which are designed for you to complete in sequence.

PART I: SELF-AWARENESS

Step One: How assertive am I?

In this section you assess your attitudes and behaviours by completing a self-perception questionnaire. The results of this questionnaire will give you an indication of how you perceive yourself regularly, frequently and/or rarely thinking, feeling and behaving.

Step Two: What does it mean to be passive, manipulative, aggressive and/or assertive?

The four different kinds of attitude and behaviour are described in Step Two and each illustrated with a case study. In each of the case studies once the person has recognized her or his non-assertive behaviour and underlying negative attitude she or he is able to develop assertive behaviour and a positive attitude towards self and others.

Step Three: Why am I as I am?

In this section you have an opportunity to reflect upon some of your early childhood experiences in terms of the kind of recognition that you received from others in the form of verbal and non-verbal messages. This will help you to understand some of your attitudes and behaviour, and help you to realize that you can change early decisions that you made about yourself and others which were, and are, negative and undermining of your self-confidence.

PART TWO: DEVELOPING ASSERTIVENESS IN YOURSELF

Step Four: Developing assertiveness through positive self-recognition

In this section you look at the kind of recognition which you give to yourself and how a negative attitude leads not only to non-assertive behaviour but also to feelings of physical discomfort, whilst a positive attitude leads to assertive behaviour and feelings of physical well-being. You also have an opportunity to look at the way in which you can turn negative into positive self-recognition and thus develop assertive behaviour.

Step Five: Developing assertiveness through giving and receiving positive recognition.

This step follows on from Step Four and gives you an opportunity to look at the kind of recognition, verbal and non-verbal, that you give to and receive from others. People tend to receive the kind of recognition from others that they give to them. Thus the more positive recognition that you give the more you will receive, the more confident you will feel and the more assertive your behaviour. The exercise encourages you to look at what you can do differently in order to receive more positive recognition from others.

Step Six: Developing assertiveness through relaxation

Being able to relax and to feel comfortable in yourself physically is a key to developing assertiveness. The person who has a positive attitude and whose behaviour is assertive is able to maintain her or his self-confidence and assertiveness through relaxing in situations in which she or he might otherwise tense up, lose confidence and behave non-assertively. The breathing exercise, described in this section, is one which you can do anywhere, and anytime!

Step Seven: Developing assertiveness through positive visualization

Linked to the ability to relax yourself physically is the ability to visualize yourself behaving assertively. All too often people enter into situations with a negative attitude towards themselves and others and anticipate a non-assertive exchange. When you prepare for a potentially difficult situation by focusing on the positive and visualizing yourself as behaving assertively you are likely to be surprised by the positive exchange and outcome!

Step Eight: Developing assertiveness through the use of appropriate communication skills

A positive attitude and assertive behaviour is about communicating effectively with others. The skills described in this section are basic communication skills, all of which depend on the skill of listening to others. There are exercises for you to do in order to practise each of the skills; however, in order to maintain assertiveness you will need to keep on practising them.

PART THREE: DEVELOPING AND MAINTAINING ASSERTIVENESS IN OTHERS

Step Nine: Developing and maintaining assertiveness in others through influencing their behaviour

In this section you look at the power of your own positive attitude and assertive behaviour to influence others' attitude and behaviour. In particular you select a colleague with whom you work who you would like to influence in order to help her or him develop assertiveness.

Step Ten: Developing and maintaining assertiveness in others through the giving and receiving of good quality feedback

There are two checklists in this section, 'Giving good quality feedback to others' and 'Receiving good quality feedback from others'. The skills of giving to and receiving good quality feedback from others are essential to managing others both effectively and assertively. Also covered in this section is the importance of regular reviewing in order not only to develop but also to maintain assertiveness in others.

Step Eleven: Developing and maintaining assertiveness in others through counselling

In this section you look at the ways in which counselling can help people to develop and maintain assertiveness. A counselling process is described, as are the necessary skills which you need to use at each stage of this counselling process.

Part I
Self-awareness

Step One
How assertive am I?

INTRODUCTION TO THE SELF-PERCEPTION
QUESTIONNAIRE

The objective of the self-perception questionnaire is to help you to identify the different ways in which you think and feel about yourself and others, and behave towards others. It is not intended to be a typology of attitudes and behaviour. Indeed, you will probably have experienced yourself in each of the four kinds of attitude and behaviour in different situations and at different times in your life. The results of the self-perception questionnaire will, however, give you an indication of the ways in which you regularly, frequently and/or rarely think and feel about yourself, and behave towards others.

Scoring instructions

1 There are eighty statements; respond with 'Yes' if the statement is *like* or *true* of you, and 'No' if the statement is *unlike* or *untrue* of you. Simply circle your response, 'Yes' or 'No'.

2 Respond to the statements as spontaneously and honestly as you can. The more honest you are with yourself the more relevant and significant will be your results.

3 Ensure that you respond to *all* the statements. It will take you approximately 5 minutes to complete the questionnaire.

4 When you have completed the questionnaire turn to the scoring chart and circle all the numbers to which you have responded 'Yes', ignore those to which you have responded 'No'.

5 You score *1 point* for each 'Yes' that you have circled.

6   Add and total your scores in the vertical columns.

7   Then turn to the section 'Interpreting your scores'. It is important that you complete the questionnaire before reading this section, otherwise it may influence how you respond to the statements.

SELF-PERCEPTION QUESTIONNAIRE

1	I have a tendency to think that others are better than me.	Yes	No
2	I am often suspicious of others' motives.	Yes	No
3	I usually rely on others to make decisions for me.	Yes	No
4	I often feel angry towards others.	Yes	No
5	I have a tendency to let others take responsibility for me.	Yes	No
6	I generally have a sense of well-being.	Yes	No
7	I often have difficulty in getting close to people.	Yes	No
8	I have a tendency to mistrust other people.	Yes	No
9	I have a tendency to keep myself to myself.	Yes	No
10	I prefer others to take the lead and for me to follow.	Yes	No
11	I usually express my feelings openly towards others.	Yes	No
12	I often assume I won't get what I want.	Yes	No
13	I often think others are after something when they thank me.	Yes	No
14	I often feel miserable.	Yes	No
15	When I ask for what I want I generally give people no choice.	Yes	No

16	I usually tell people rather than ask them to do things.	Yes	No
17	I have a tendency to blame others when things go wrong.	Yes	No
18	I seek others' views when making decisions which affect them.	Yes	No
19	I have a tendency to put myself down.	Yes	No
20	When asked I often don't know what I want.	Yes	No
21	I am usually cautious about what I say to others about myself.	Yes	No
22	I usually listen to and take account of others' views.	Yes	No
23	I generally enjoy getting on with my work.	Yes	No
24	I usually deal with conflict situations directly.	Yes	No
25	I rarely say 'No' when asked to do something.	Yes	No
26	I have a tendency to be sarcastic.	Yes	No
27	I usually have difficulty in delegating to others.	Yes	No
28	I generally have creative solutions to problems.	Yes	No
29	When I refuse a request I usually feel guilty.	Yes	No
30	I have a tendency to be anxious about what people think of me.	Yes	No
31	I generally avoid taking on responsibility.	Yes	No
32	I have a tendency to see others as more important than me.	Yes	No
33	I am generally quick to feel criticized.	Yes	No

34	I often think I am the only one who can do the job correctly.	Yes	No
35	I generally deal with conflict situations indirectly.	Yes	No
36	I usually enjoy discussing ideas with people.	Yes	No
37	I rarely give praise to others.	Yes	No
38	I usually find it difficult to sort out my problems.	Yes	No
39	I rarely receive feedback about my behaviour.	Yes	No
40	I regularly appreciate others for what they have done.	Yes	No
41	I am often acknowledged by others for what I do.	Yes	No
42	I have a tendency to be inconsistent about what I tell people.	Yes	No
43	I am generally quick to criticize others.	Yes	No
44	I am often easily hurt by others.	Yes	No
45	I usually let others make decisions for me.	Yes	No
46	I am often hostile towards people.	Yes	No
47	I am often short-tempered with people.	Yes	No
48	I usually enjoy getting involved with and committed to tasks.	Yes	No
49	I generally take account of others' needs and wants.	Yes	No
50	I have a tendency to avoid eye contact.	Yes	No
51	I often feel resentful towards others.	Yes	No
52	I rarely ask for what I want.	Yes	No

53	I usually assume that I won't get what I want.	Yes	No
54	I have a tendency to feel lonely.	Yes	No
55	I often feel that others have let me down.	Yes	No
56	I usually ask questions in order to gather information.	Yes	No
57	I generally check out my assumptions with the people concerned.	Yes	No
58	I try not to offend other people.	Yes	No
59	I often fantasize about ways of getting my own back on others.	Yes	No
60	I usually tell people what I think.	Yes	No
61	I generally say sorry when I have made a mistake.	Yes	No
62	I readily accept that people will say 'No' to me sometimes.	Yes	No
63	I have a tendency to jump to and draw conclusions.	Yes	No
64	I rarely tell others what I really think or feel.	Yes	No
65	I usually go along with what other people want.	Yes	No
66	I usually feel inferior to others.	Yes	No
67	I am frequently demotivated in my work.	Yes	No
68	I am often despondent about things in general.	Yes	No
69	I have a tendency to dismiss others' wants and needs.	Yes	No
70	I usually respect other people irrespective of their views.	Yes	No
71	I readily take on responsibility.	Yes	No

72	I am quick to put other peoples' ideas down.	Yes	No
73	I am usually anxious about upsetting other people.	Yes	No
74	I regularly seek feedback from other people.	Yes	No
75	I am usually keen to spot the flaws in others' arguments.	Yes	No
76	I often have negative thoughts about myself and others.	Yes	No
77	I usually feel equal to others.	Yes	No
78	I often expect that people will dislike me.	Yes	No
79	I have a tendency to be put upon by others.	Yes	No
80	I usually assume that others will not get on with me.	Yes	No

Scoring chart

Passive	Manipulative	Aggressive	Assertive
1	2	4	6
3	7	9	11
5	8	12	18
10	13	15	22
19	14	16	23
20	21	17	24
25	26	27	28
29	31	33	36
30	35	34	40
32	38	37	41

Passive	Manipulative	Aggressive	Assertive
44	42	39	48
45	46	43	49
52	50	47	56
53	54	51	57
58	59	55	61
65	64	60	62
66	67	63	70
73	68	69	71
78	76	72	74
79	80	75	77

Interpreting your scores

Scores 14-20, suggest that this is how you regularly think and feel about yourself and others, and behave towards them.

Scores 7-13, suggest that this is how you frequently think and feel about yourself and others, and behave towards them.

Scores 0-6, suggest that this is how you rarely think and feel about yourself and others, and behave towards them.

Understanding your scores: Key characteristics of the four attitudes and behaviours

The four different attitudes and behaviour are Passive, Manipulative, Aggressive and Assertive. Your range of scores gives you an indication of the ways in which you tend to think and feel about yourself and others, and behave towards others regularly, frequently and/or rarely.

Your highest score may be Assertive, in which case you may think that this book is not, after all, for you! You may, however, find it useful to look at your next highest score and consider in what situations you experience yourself behaving in that way. For example, your next highest score may be Aggressive. Many people who consider themselves to be assertive most of the time recognize that when they are under pressure and/or in a stressful situation their behaviour changes and they become aggressive.

If your highest score is not Assertive then this book is for you. Now that you have identified your non-assertive attitudes and behaviours you can start to explore and understand your attitudes and behaviours with a view to developing self-confidence, a positive attitude and assertive behaviour.

Listed below are some of the key characteristics of each of the four different attitudes and behaviours. In *Step Two: What does it mean to be passive, manipulative, aggressive and/or assertive?* a detailed description is given of each of the four types of attitude and behaviour, and the Life Position underlying each of them.

Key characteristics of a negative attitude and passive behaviour
If your highest score, or one of your highest scores, is Passive then some or all of the following characteristics are likely to be true of you:

■ lack of self-confidence and low self-esteem
■ lack of self-respect
■ self put-downs
■ negative feelings and thoughts about yourself
■ feelings of inferiority compared to others
■ like others to be in control of people and situations
■ feel guilty towards others
■ demotivated

Key characteristics of a negative attitude and manipulative behaviour
If your highest score, or one of your highest scores, is Manipulative then some or all of the following characteristics are likely to be true of you:

■ lack of self-confidence and low self-esteem
■ lack of self-respect and lack of respect for others
■ mistrustful and suspicious of others' motives
■ negative feelings and thoughts about self and others
■ feel very wary towards others
■ dishonest and indirect
■ twist what others have said

undermine others' self-esteem
depressed and demotivated

Key characteristics of a negative attitude and aggressive behaviour
If your highest score, or one of your highest scores, is Aggressive then some or all of the following characteristics are likely to be true of you:

lack of self-confidence and low self-esteem
lack of respect towards others
put others down
feelings of superiority
like to be in control of people and situations
disinterested in others' thoughts and feelings
feel angry towards others and are quick to blame them
don't listen to or ask others questions
dismissive of feedback

Key characteristics of a positive attitude and assertive behaviour
If your highest score, or one of your high scores, is Assertive then some or all of the following characteristics are likely to be true of you:

self-confidence and high self-esteem
respect for self and towards others
take responsibility for self
motivated to do a good job
interested in others' feelings and thoughts
ask questions
honest and direct
listen to others
ask others for feedback

THE NEXT STEP

Now that you have identified your particular attitude and behaviours you are ready to find out what it means to be passive, manipulative, aggressive and/or assertive.

Step Two
What does it mean to be passive, manipulative, aggressive and/or assertive?

The key characteristics which the three non-assertive attitudes and behaviours have in common are a lack of self-confidence and low self-esteem. If you have diagnosed yourself to be passive, manipulative or aggressive then you are likely to experience yourself as lacking in confidence and self-worth. What distinguishes and differentiates the person who is assertive is her or his self-confidence and feelings of self-worth.

THE FOUR LIFE POSITIONS

The person who has a positive attitude about herself or himself, and a positive attitude towards others and her or his environment can be said to have a healthy Life Position. A Life Position is, as the term suggests, a position for life; however, a person who has a negative attitude towards herself or himself and others can, by becoming conscious of it, change it to a positive attitude. There are four Life Positions, each of which corresponds to one of the four types of attitude and behaviour as follows:

1 *Passive*: I'm not OK – You're OK
2 *Manipulative*: I'm not OK – You're not OK
3 *Aggressive*: I'm OK – You're not OK
4 *Assertive*: I'm OK – You're OK

Life Positions are sometimes known as 'attitudes of the moment' since you move between these positions depending on the situation you are in and the kind of thoughts and feelings you are experiencing at the time. An 'attitude of the moment' does not, however, detract from your underlying Life Position about which you made an unconscious decision in the early years of your life. You can, however, change your negative Life Position to the positive *I'm OK – You're OK* Life Position by consciously challenging your early decision and by making a new decision.

The only healthy Life Position is *I'm OK – You're OK* and it is this Position which underlies the assertive attitude and behaviour. The theory of Transactional Analysis suggests that by the end of the first year of our lives most of us have unconsciously made the decision *I'm not OK – You're OK*. This *not OK* decision is made as a result of our being dependent on others for our well-being, and most significantly our being dependent on others for our feelings of self-worth and self-respect. By the time we are 3 years old we have usually made a firm, albeit unconscious, decision as to our Life Position. Unless this decision is consciously challenged it will influence us for the rest of our lives.

If, as a child, you were not given positive recognition by your parents and/or those who looked after you, then your feelings about yourself are likely to have been negative. Indeed we are very dependent on our carers having a positive attitude and behaviour towards themselves and others; if, for example, your parents, or carers, didn't show each other or you respect it is unlikely that you grew up feeling valued and respected by them. These early experiences of yourself influence how you feel, think and behave for the rest of your life; it is, however, possible to change how you feel and think about yourself and others and to change your behaviour. In *Step Three: Why am I as I am?* you have an opportunity to explore some of your early childhood memories and to understand why you are as you are, before going on to look at ways in which you can develop self-confidence and assertiveness.

The following descriptions of the four types of behaviours are each illustrated by a case study. The case studies show the impact of a person's Life Position on her or his attitude and behaviour towards self and others. They also illustrate very clearly how a person's attitude and behaviour influences that of other people. In each of the case studies the person decides to change her or his attitude and behaviour from non-assertive to assertive. Irrespective of your self-diagnosis from the self-perception questionnaire, I suggest that you read through all the descriptions and case studies so that you can recognize the different attitudes and behaviours in your self, and in others.

PASSIVE ATTITUDE AND BEHAVIOUR: I'M NOT OK – YOU'RE OK

The person whose attitude and behaviour is passive lacks confidence in herself or himself. People who are lacking in self-confidence tend to compare themselves to others and to find themselves lacking by comparison. They are likely to invite negative recognition from others which confirms their negative view of themselves. All too often they find people to put them down whose attitude and behaviour is aggressive. People whose attitude and behaviour is aggressive tend to cope with their lack of self-confidence by putting others down and so the passive person is often a sitting target. This symbiotic relationship is further discussed under aggressive behaviour.

The *I'm not OK – You're OK* Life Position is unconsciously decided upon by the child in the early years of life, often leading to the child complying with her or his parents' requests and/or rebelling against them. Whilst healthy adaptation is an important part of socialization, compliance due to a lack of self-esteem is demotivating and can potentially lead a person to behave manipulatively.

Self-perception

If you have diagnosed your attitude and behaviour to be passive then you are probably aware of your lack of self-confidence. A lack of confidence in yourself has far-reaching consequences for you since you tend to avoid taking on responsibility and/or committing to ideas or people. Instead of committing yourself to ideas and people you end up complying with them. You are likely to experience others as making too many demands of you and to find it difficult to either say 'No' or to make requests. One of the first steps in moving towards developing self-confidence is for you to realize that you are responsible for yourself and that you can influence others through your own behaviour.

In *Step Three: Why am I as I am?* you will have an opportunity to explore your underlying Life Position before looking at ways in which you can develop assertiveness.

Read the case study which follows and you will see how Sally began to develop her self-confidence and to change her behaviour from passive to assertive.

Case study

Sally is a regional manager for a multinational retail company. She enjoyed her job, in particular talking with people on a one-to-one basis. A large part of her job, however, involved attending meetings at which she always felt self-conscious and at which she usually felt threatened.

At meetings Sally tended to withdraw into herself, maintaining a silence. She would sit quietly, on the one hand hoping that someone would notice her silence and invite her to comment, and on the other hand dreading that she would be asked to express a point of view. Her experience of meetings had resulted in her feeling personally challenged and/or criticized whenever she expressed her own opinions. She tended not to voice either disagreement or agreement with other people's views, preferring to maintain silence and keep a low profile. In this way she hoped that she would avoid any potentially difficult discussions which may involve her in conflict with others.

She noticed that whenever she did attempt to contribute to a discussion that other people ignored and/or appeared to be irritated with her. This confirmed her thinking that it was best to keep quiet and that her experience was, compared to that of the others', irrelevant despite the fact that she had worked for a number of retail companies prior to this job.

She communicated her decision to maintain a silence, non-verbally by doodling, keeping her head down and by not making eye contact with anyone. By the end of these meetings she often had a headache and herself felt irritable.

David, her boss, occasionally attended the meetings and had observed her withdrawn behaviour. When Sally requested to be absent from one of the meetings, having already been absent from several others, David decided to talk with her about her behaviour. Initially Sally responded to his questions defensively, suggesting that the reason for her lack of contribution was due to the others' behaviour. She complained that they wouldn't let her express her views and that when she did she was ignored by them.

David commented that her non-verbal behaviour led him to

think that she was disinterested in the topics under discussion. In particular her lack of eye contact and her keeping her head down suggested to him, and probably to the others, that she was avoiding them and also avoiding taking responsibility for any of the decisions which were being taken. He pointed out to her that her silence was a form of contribution which had an impact on the others. He himself confessed to feeling irritated by her silence and non-verbal behaviour.

Sally was surprised and concerned to realize that her silence could be having an opposite impact to the one which she desired. She discussed with David the reasons for her withdrawn behaviour, in particular her lack of self-confidence. For as long as she could remember she had compared herself with others and decided that her views were not as important as theirs. She realized that this had led her to think of herself as worthless, especially in group situations in which everyone else had so much more to contribute than her. Sally's underlying Life Position was *I'm not OK – You're OK*.

Once Sally had recognized the way in which she compared herself with others and how she perceived them as always being better than herself she was able to look at ways of developing her self-worth. David commented on how much more relaxed she appeared to be on a one-to-one basis, and gave her feedback on her non-verbal behaviour. In a one-to-one situation Sally knew that she looked at and listened to the person with whom she was talking. She felt that the person was interested in her and she would freely express her views to her or him. For Sally this was the beginning of developing her self-confidence and behaving assertively.

When she next attended a regional meeting she made a conscious effort to look at people when they were talking and to look around at people. After several meetings she began to contribute verbally and was delighted that people responded to her with interest. She was able to separate her opinion from herself so that on the occasions when her opinions were challenged or criticized she did not feel personally criticized.

MANIPULATIVE ATTITUDE AND BEHAVIOUR: I'M NOT OK – YOU'RE NOT OK

A person whose attitude and behaviour is manipulative has a negative opinion of herself or himself and of others. Her or his behaviour is self-destructive and destructive towards others. The person is usually depressed and demotivated. Many people have experienced themselves moving into this Life Position *I'm not OK – You're not OK* during a major transition in their lives. In particular, managers who have not been consulted about a decision which directly affects them have reported feeling very negative about themselves and towards the organization.

Examples which managers have given include the decision of a company to move the manager from one site to another, involving uprooting the family and the loss of friends both for the parents and the children; or the anticipation of promotion followed by the unexpectedness of not being promoted and/or of being demoted.

A common example in times of takeovers and rationalizations is that of redundancy. Despite the generous redundancy packages offered by some companies the redundant person naturally feels rejected by the company. The realization for some managers that their long-standing service and commitment has not been reciprocated by the company can lead them to feeling extremely negative towards themselves and the company.

Self-perception

If you have diagnosed yourself as manipulative then you are probably aware of your lack of self-confidence. Your perception of yourself suggests that you find it difficult to trust others, indeed you may well find it difficult to trust yourself. You are likely to suspect and expect others to be somewhat devious with you and to experience yourself as being devious with them. You are also probably aware of having negative thoughts and feelings about yourself and towards others. A manipulative attitude and behaviour is both self-destructive and devisive towards others. Whether you made the decision *I'm not OK – You're not OK* in the first years of your life or you are currently experiencing many changes in your life, some of which you feel are out of your control, it is important to remember that you can change your attitude and behaviour to being assertive. You will find *Step Three: Why am I as I am?* useful in helping you to understand your attitude and behaviour and the exercises on 'Developing assertiveness through positive self-recognition' particularly useful.

Read the case study which follows and you will see how Victor was able to change his attitude and behaviour from manipulative to assertive.

Case study

Victor is a marketing manager for a computer company. He has worked for the same company for several years; prior to his current job he was a sales consultant. He enjoyed selling software far more than he enjoys managing. He particularly liked the amount of travelling which was involved in his previous job. He has no family commitments, having been divorced sometime ago and his son being at college.

One of the reasons for the change of job, and sideways move, was due to him not meeting his targets over a fairly lengthy period of time. Victor felt extremely angry towards his old and new bosses. He said that his old boss had not warned him in advance of the job change and that his new boss treated him as if he was incapable of taking on any responsibilities. He resented not having the freedom to make decisions on his own and found it difficult to relate to the other members of the marketing team. He felt that he couldn't trust them and that they, like his new boss, didn't rate him or his abilities. He in turn viewed them as upstarts and lacking in the kind of experience which he had to offer from his previous position, but which he chose not to offer.

Victor's new boss, Terry, had talked to him but found it extremely difficult to communicate with him. As a result, Terry assumed that it was best to leave Victor to get on with the job and for him to consult Terry only when a decision was to be made. Terry knew that this strategy wasn't working well since Victor had avoided consulting him on a recent decision and on another occasion had denied having taken a decision that had resulted in a client withdrawing their account from the company. Terry was also concerned about Victor's increasing time off.

Terry confronted Victor on the issue of time-keeping and asked him if there were any reasons for his lateness not only to work but also to important meetings. Victor argued that his lateness was no different from that of his colleagues who, like himself, had important things to attend to both on and off site. Victor denied that there was a problem and complained about the time he spent having to wait around to discuss issues when he could be getting on with the job.

Terry decided to seek outside advice since he felt unable to deal with Victor who was making life difficult not only for himself but also for the rest of the team. Terry knew that some of the team members did not like working with Victor, preferring to work on their own, whilst others obviously felt that Victor had been wronged by the company and supported him in his angry outbursts. The result was that the team's morale was very low, and Terry suspected that some of the team of whom he thought highly would start to move on to other positions within the company.

The advice Terry took was that Victor should be offered professional counselling by the company on a private and confidential basis. Terry could not imagine Victor agreeing to the offer. However, after a series of events, one of which involved him in a brawl with a colleague, Victor realized that unless he accepted the offer and changed his behaviour he would be without a job.

Victor had an extremely low opinion of himself and others, his attitude and behaviour were manipulative. His lack of self-respect and self-esteem had resulted in various forms of self-destructive behaviour. One of the main reasons for his being moved from the job as sales consultant was his drinking, which had resulted in him losing his driving licence. His old boss had fought hard to give Victor another chance and had hoped that the new job would solve the problem. However, Victor found himself drinking more rather than less, especially on his own at home or in pubs, but denied that he had a drink problem. It was after a lunchtime drink that he had had an emotional outburst and hit a colleague.

Another characteristic typical of Victor's manipulative behaviour was his not taking responsibility for himself and his actions and blaming them on others. He was quick to find fault with others and felt that no one could be trusted. His behaviour was therefore not only self-destructive but also destructive of the team. Victor's self-recognition was negative; he felt angry and resentful most of the time. He expressed his feelings by behaving in ways which not only could potentially hurt himself but also others, such as fast driving after drinking over the limit. Rather than change his behaviour his negative attitude meant that he always blamed others and denied any criticisms.

This Life Position *I'm not OK – You're not OK* is the most destructive of all Life Positions. Sometimes after a particularly traumatic life experience a person whose basic Life Position is *I'm not OK – You're OK* moves into this manipulative Life Position.

In Victor's case a combination of potentially difficult situations, including the separation and divorce, and his estrangement from his son had led Victor to feel worthless. The sideways move in his job had only compounded his negative thoughts about himself and towards others, resulting in moving from the *I'm not OK – You're OK* to the *I'm not OK – You're not OK* Life Position.

Initially Victor was reluctant to change his attitude and behaviour but, motivated by the desire to keep his job and to make contact with his son again, he committed himself to counselling for a limited number of sessions. The counselling helped Victor to understand how his negative attitudes and behaviour were impacting on others and also how he could begin to develop self-confidence and a positive self-image.

He realized that as a child he had tended to keep himself to himself, and as a result of moving from school to school had never made any long-lasting friends. He remembered being viewed with suspicion by other children and the difficulty he had had making friends with them. He had preferred his previous job because it involved travelling. His marriage had suffered in the same way as his job from his lack of trust.

Victor's move towards the *I'm OK – You're OK* Life Position was slow and difficult for him, particularly so since he and the people with whom he worked had got used to his manipulative behaviour. After a couple of counselling sessions Victor agreed to talk with Terry, his boss, and ask him to give him regular feedback on his behaviour. In particular he asked for feedback on his positive behaviour. He also agreed to give positive feedback to his colleagues and was surprised what a difference it made to his relationships with them. At the end of the series of counselling sessions Victor decided to join a sports club where he could meet people and get fit at the same time.

AGGRESSIVE ATTITUDE AND BEHAVIOUR: I'M OK – YOU'RE NOT OK

Assertive behaviour is frequently confused with aggressive behaviour. Managers often describe the sort of person they view as being assertive as someone who 'gets things done', 'knows what they want and goes for it'. Whilst these are true of the person who is behaving assertively, all too often she or he is someone whose style of managing is one that they do not respect, because the person gets things done by telling people what to do and goes for what they want without respecting or considering the views of others.

Managers are often surprised that underlying aggressive behaviour and the *I'm not OK – You're not OK* Life Position is a lack of self-confidence and that this Position is indeed a way of coping with the basic decision and Life Position *I'm not OK – You're OK*. Understanding this can be of enormous help when dealing with people who appear to be aggressive and also when you recognize your behaviour as aggressive.

There is a symbiotic relationship between aggressive and passive behaviours. Very often people whose Life Position is *I'm not OK – You're OK* attract people whose Life Position is *I'm OK – You're not OK* and vice versa, since people whose attitude and behaviour is passive think that everyone else is better than them, and those whose attitude and behaviour is aggressive think that they are better than everyone else.

Self-perception

If you have diagnosed yourself as aggressive you are probably aware of your lack of self-confidence. You hide your inner lack of self-confidence by behaving aggressively towards others. Your attitude towards others tends to be defensive; you imagine that people are 'out to get you' in some way and that you have to protect yourself from them. Although the underlying Life Position of aggressive behaviour is *I'm OK – You're not OK* this Position and behaviour are often a way of managing a lack of self-confidence and an *I'm not OK – You're OK* Life Position. One of the ways in which you manage your lack of self-confidence is to compare yourself to others, to put them down and to feel better than them. As a result of this behaviour you may well feel better in yourself for a while; however, feelings of self-worth which are experienced at others' expense are usually short-lived and rather superficial.

You will find *Step Three: Why am I as I am?* useful in helping you to understand your attitude and behaviour before going on to looking at ways in which you can develop and maintain assertiveness.

Read the case study which follows and notice in particular how, once she recognizes her aggressive behaviour, Karen is able to change her attitude and behaviour to assertive.

Case study

Karen is a conference manager at an international hotel. She is extremely well-qualified for her job, having obtained a degree in Business Studies and having several years' experience working for different international hotels. Karen prefers working with people to doing administration. One of the difficulties she experienced in her previous job as general manager of a conference centre was the administrative work. She was attracted to the job of conference manager because it involved not only managing the conference facilities but also leading and building a team.

At a time of increasing competition with other hotels offering similar conference facilities Karen was extremely keen for the conference centre to establish itself as the best and for it to make a profit. She was also determined to make her mark and build her own reputation as a manager in the business. She already had a reputation for being a hard worker and indeed often worked in her own time.

Although Karen preferred working with people to doing administrative work she experienced herself as being alienated from her team, most of whom she had been working with for over a year. She found it difficult to delegate work to the senior managers in the team despite the fact that she had herself recruited them. Karen decided that the team would benefit from a team-building event. She imagined that they would welcome the opportunity to spend time together as a team but was concerned as to whether her presence would be inhibiting for them. In the event it was agreed that it was important for her to attend since she was indeed a member of the team.

Up until the team building event Karen had considered herself to be an assertive person. She was strong-minded and expressed her views clearly. Once she had made up her mind as to a course of action she committed to it and expected everyone else to agree with her. On the occasions when her views were challenged she quickly defended her position.

Karen consulted the team on decisions which affected them and the future of the conference centre but rarely changed her mind. The rest of the team considered it futile to contribute to discussions when their views were different from Karen's. They would go along with what she wanted and complain to each other afterwards about the decision. This had the effect of bringing them closer together and, as Karen had experienced, of alienating her.

The team perceived Karen to be assertive in an aggressive way. They talked to her about how they admired her commitment to the job and how they felt that they were merely the means by which she could achieve her desired success. They did not feel valued or appreciated by her. Indeed they thought that she only noticed a person when she or he made a mistake. Prior to the team building event none of them would have ventured to give Karen feedback on her behaviour towards them, fearing that they would lose their jobs.

Karen and the team were surprised to realize that underlying her hard exterior was someone lacking in self-confidence, so much so that she protected herself from feedback by asserting her views in such a way that no one questioned them. Her self-protection enabled her to keep people at a distance. In this way she managed to conceal her underlying lack of self-confidence and lack of self-worth.

She rarely appreciated others for their efforts and in turn didn't expect to be appreciated by them for her efforts. The members of the team realized that whilst they looked for appreciation from her they had not considered that Karen herself would benefit from their appreciation.

Despite the success in her job she always felt that she could have done a better job and focused her attention on what had not gone well or was not going well. As a result she focused on other people's mistakes and on what she considered should be done better. She perceived other people to be the problem and usually thought she could have done a better job herself, if only she'd had the time.

Karen's underlying Life Position was *I'm not OK – You're OK*. Over the years she had learnt to cope with her lack of self-confidence and feelings of worthlessness by adopting the *I'm OK – You're not OK* Life Position. She compared herself to others and competed with them. She defended herself by always being right and the others being wrong. It turned out that whilst she wanted to be part of the team she was wary of them and of any closeness. She imagined that they, like herself, were comparing and competing with her and that she had to defend herself at all costs.

The team agreed as a whole that they all needed to develop their self-confidence and to trust one another more. In particular they recognized the need to give each other positive feedback and also to ask for it from each other. Karen agreed that what she wanted from them was their commitment to ideas and actions rather than compliance. She realized that this meant she would have to listen to the team's views and that she would not always be able to pursue her own course of action.

Several months after the initial team building event the team had a review at which Karen reported how much more creative they were as a team. The team expressed how they were more committed and motivated and that they perceived Karen as more relaxed and assertive. Karen said that she was more confident in herself and that most of the time she experienced herself as behaving assertively. The occasions on which she behaved aggressively or defensively were when she was under pressure or felt herself to be under threat.

ASSERTIVE ATTITUDE AND BEHAVIOUR, I'M OK – YOU'RE OK

The assertive Life Position *I'm OK – You're OK* is a conscious decision, whereas the other three negative Life Positions are made unconsciously and non-verbally by the child.

Once you are aware of your early unconscious decision you can change it to the positive and assertive fourth Life Position. This is not to say that your attitude will always be positive nor that your behaviour will always be assertive; however, you will be aware of the difference not only in how you feel and think about yourself and others but also what impact your behaviour is having on people. Also, having recognized your own early decision, and having made the decision to change, you will be able to help others recognize and change their own negative Life Position to the positive Life Position.

What motivates people to change? The process of transition is difficult for many people. It usually involves taking risks as well as giving up and letting go of attitudes and behaviours of which we are either unaware or of which we are secretly fond. The impact of our changed attitude and behaviour on others can also involve further changes, as people with whom we previously colluded are challenged by our behaviour – for example, in the symbiotic relationship between two people who have, respectively, the *I'm OK – You're not OK* and *I'm not OK – You're OK* Life Positions.

When you feel confident in yourself and are focusing on positive thoughts and feelings your behaviour will be assertive; your assertive behaviour will in turn challenge others to change their behaviour and to respond differently to you.

One of the problems managers frequently express is that whilst their behaviour is different and more assertive it is everyone else who needs to change their behaviour. Through changing your own attitudes and behaviour you can influence the attitudes and behaviour of others; you cannot change as such the attitudes and behaviour of others, only influence. This is the power of your own attitudes and behaviour as a manager on everyone with whom you interact.

Read the case study below in which Tim, whose attitude and behaviour was passive, used some of the exercises and skills of self-assertion described in this book to change his attitude and behaviour to assertive.

Self-perception

If you have diagnosed yourself as assertive then you are probably aware of feeling confident in yourself most of the time. You are also probably aware of situations in which you tend to lack confidence and of behaving non-assertively in them. It is useful to recognize the negative attitude and non-assertive behaviour which you tend to adopt when you are lacking in confidence. Many managers who have a positive attitude and whose behaviour is for the most part assertive find that under pressure their behaviour becomes aggressive. Once you recognize your negative attitude and non-assertive behaviour you can consciously choose to think positively and to behave assertively.

Case study

Tim works for a design company and is manager of the Research and Development team. He joined the company having had a variety of jobs with other design companies following his training. Tim enjoys his work for the most part; however, as happened in his previous jobs he began to feel bored by the work. He didn't want to leave the job since he had only recently moved into a house which needed renovating. His intention to start work on the house as soon as he moved in had not materialized since he felt so exhausted when he returned from work.

He declined invitations to go out with friends and had stopped calling on friends at weekends because he always planned to be working on the house, although somehow he never got round to it. Tim had been a keen jogger but since his move he had lost his jogging partner and had not found anyone else keen to join him. Without the encouragement and support of a fellow jogger Tim lacked the motivation and discipline to go jogging on his own. Tim's boss and colleagues commented to each other that he seemed to be at a low ebb; they respected his privacy and didn't like to ask him what, if anything, was wrong, suspecting that he had difficulties at home. Eventually Tim decided that he needed to take some time off work to get his house and himself sorted out. His boss, Liz, agreed to the time off hoping that the break would make the difference to Tim's performance at work. Tim explained that he was finding it difficult to motivate himself and others and that he quickly felt tired and weary. He avoided telling Liz that he felt terribly bored by the work, and with himself. He felt that he had lost his creative spark but didn't want to risk his job by admitting to it.

Liz, who herself had experienced great doubts in herself and her creative abilities, asked Tim if he had ever felt the same sort of weariness in previous jobs. Tim confessed that he had and that his way of dealing with it had been to change jobs. He realized that this only temporarily solved his feelings of boredom and tiredness, and that he would really like to find another way of overcoming these negative feelings and thoughts.

As a result of talking to Liz, Tim attended a self-development course for managers on improving personal effectiveness. He received feedback from people on the course and encouragement to look at the kind of self-recognition he gave himself and the kind of recognition that he had been given as a child.

Tim's early decision had been *I'm not OK – You're OK* and it was this underlying lack of self-confidence which resulted in him always feeling that he wasn't good enough for the job and that someone would sooner or later find out that he was a fraud. His way of coping was to withdraw from the people with whom he worked and to lose interest in his work in order to protect himself from any criticism which he felt sure he would receive. Indeed he realized that he actually asked for criticism from people in order to confirm his view of himself.

Tim was initially rather sceptical of positive affirmations and of visualizing himself fit and healthy but agreed to give it a go. He returned to work feeling much more positive about himself and more sure of his abilities. Instead of imagining that everyone was in some way out to get him he reminded himself that they were likely to have the same kind of doubts about themselves and their work as he had, and that just as he needed positive encouragement from them they needed it from him. Initially he felt awkward when he appreciated the work of individuals in his team. He thought that they would think he was after something, especially the women. However, he felt more relaxed and enjoyed his work much more, focusing less and less on the negative things. Much to his surprise he found that as he focused more on the positive so too did other team members.

Tim's behaviour was noticeably assertive; he contributed ideas in group discussions whereas previously he had held back, assuming that his ideas would either be knocked down or totally ignored by his colleagues. He also encouraged others to contribute their ideas and actively looked for ways in which they could be developed and/or actioned.

The impact of Tim's self-confidence and assertive behaviour on his colleagues meant not only that they had more fun together bouncing ideas around, but also that they were able to acknowledge to one another when they needed help with an idea, something which they hadn't previously done.

SUMMARY

The theory of Life Positions is a useful way of looking at the difference between non-assertive and assertive behaviours. If you perceive yourself as assertive your underlying Life Position is *I'm OK – You're OK*; you feel secure in your self-worth, you are self-confident and have self-respect as well as a respect for others. Whilst most people are assertive some of the time, many of us experience ourselves as having a non-assertive, negative attitude and behaviour often when in stressful situations and/or under pressure.

The theory of Life Positions suggests that by the age of twelve months we make an unconscious decision as to our Life Position, for most of us this decision is *I'm not OK – You're OK*; in other words we lack self-esteem and self-confidence. By the time we are three years old we have found ways of coping with our lack of self-confidence and unconsciously decided either that *I'm not OK – You're OK, I'm not OK – You're not OK* or *I'm OK – You're not OK*.

You can change your attitude and behaviour from non-assertive to assertive by making a conscious decision *I'm OK – You're OK*. When you make this conscious decision you are challenging your negative attitudes about yourself and others. This book is about helping you to develop self-confidence, to develop an *I'm OK – You're OK* Life Position and assertive behaviour. Once you have developed assertiveness in yourself you will be able, as a manager, to help others develop assertiveness in themselves.

The next step is for you to explore your underlying Life Position and to understand 'Why am I as I am?'.

Step Three
Why am I as I am?

In this section you have an opportunity to reflect upon your early childhood experience and memories of:

■ recognition, in the form of non-verbal and verbal messages, that you received as a child;
■ decisions that you made about yourself and others as a consequence of the messages you received, and to look at how these decisions influence your attitude and behaviour now.

RECOGNITION

Some years ago I watched an interview of a woman who described her success in life as being due to her mother having given her the confidence to be herself as a child. The phrase 'confidence to be herself' struck me then, and now, as being a gift from which we would all benefit. The woman described how her mother had encouraged her from an early age to try things out for herself, and to find her own way of being and doing things. This, she said, had enabled her both to assert herself and to be creative.

Many of us are not given the encouragement to discover and to be ourselves. Indeed many children lose confidence in themselves through simply not being allowed to experiment with different ways of doing things, through not being listened to, and through not being consulted about things which directly affect them.

As a consequence children find various ways of coping, some by withdrawing into themselves to the extent of not asking questions or expressing their thoughts and feelings about themselves and things, and others by bullying and shouting to be heard to get what they want. These ways of coping stay with us, albeit in more sophisticated forms, into adulthood, resulting in non-assertive behaviour, a lack of creativity and demotivation.

RECOGNITION IN THE FORM OF NON-VERBAL AND VERBAL MESSAGES THAT YOU RECEIVED AS A CHILD

Recognition in the form of messages refers to pieces of information which were communicated to you by your parents and/or primary carers verbally and non-verbally about yourself, others and life in general. Some of the messages which you received as a child were probably negative and others positive. If you received a lot of positive messages about yourself, others and life then the chances are that your underlying Life Position was and is *I'm OK – You're OK*. Conversely, if you received a lot of negative messages then your Life Position is likely to be either *I'm not OK – You're OK, I'm not OK – You're not OK*, or *I'm OK – You're not OK*.

The process of remembering and reflecting upon the kinds of messages that you received about yourself and others as a child will enable you to make conscious some of the hitherto unconscious decisions that you made about yourself and others. Once you have an understanding of the decisions that you made as a child you can begin to assess their value to you now and, if appropriate, to develop more positive attitudes about yourself and others which will lead to greater self-confidence and to assertive behaviour.

Negative recognition

Negative recognition in the form of messages about yourself can be communicated non-verbally and verbally; they are about who you are as a person, about your behaviour or performance.

Negative non-verbal messages include:

■ no physical contact
■ physical punishment in the form of being slapped and/or hit
■ being talked about and referred to, but being ignored

Negative non-verbal messages in the early years of a child's life have an enormous impact on how children feel about themselves. The baby and young child experience so much of the environment through their physical senses, through touching, seeing, hearing, smelling and tasting. Their self-perception is thus very much based on their experience of themselves physically. In a world in which everyone else, and everything, is bigger by comparison the child needs a lot of physical support and encouragement in order to develop self-confidence and a positive self-image.

A child who receives physical punishment and/or very little positive physical contact from the very people she or he is dependent on for physical nourishment learns not to trust others, to believe that the world is an unsafe place to be, and that she or he needs to protect herself or himself from being hurt.

Negative verbal messages include:

'Don't ask "why?" just do it ...'
'Don't do that ...'
'Don't be so stupid ...'
'If you don't stop that then ...'
'Boys don't cry ...'
'Girls don't shout ...'
'Stop it immediately or else ...'
'You'll never be any good at it ...'
'You can't do that ...'

Negative verbal messages are often characterized by beginning with 'Don't' or 'Can't'. If a child receives mostly 'Don't' messages then she or he learns from others 'Don't be yourself' and 'Don't do what you're doing'. Many negative verbal messages are characterized by a threat, 'If you don't do what I'm asking then ...'. A child who receives a lot of 'Can't' messages ends up thinking and feeling that she or he 'Can't' be herself or himself, or experiment with things.

Messages which are about you as a person, rather than your behaviour, are often generalized and in the form of a put-down, for example, 'You are stupid'. As a result of these negative verbal messages the child begins to believe that she or he is 'stupid', 'naughty' or 'silly'.

Negative non-verbal and verbal messages result in the child feeling that what she or he thinks and feels is unimportant and indeed that she or he is unimportant and worthless. The child's experience of school often confirms this view of self. She or he is not encouraged to ask questions or to experiment with different ways of doing things. There tends to be a 'right' way of going about things. All too often the child is punished for doing something 'wrong' when in fact she or he was simply doing something in a different way.

EXERCISE: RECOGNIZING THE NEGATIVE MESSAGES YOU RECEIVED AS A CHILD

What were the negative messages that you received from your parents and/or primary carers during your childhood (0–12 years old)?

Negative non-verbal messages:

Negative verbal messages:

What decisions about yourself and others do you remember making as a child as a result of the negative non-verbal and verbal messages that you received from your parents and/or primary carers?

Negative decisions about myself:

Negative decisions about others:

How do these decisions influence your attitude and behaviour now?

Positive recognition

Positive recognition about yourself as a person and your behaviour can, like negative messages, be communicated non-verbally and verbally. Positive messages can be about you as a person irrespective of your behaviour and they can be about your behaviour or performance.

A child who receives mostly positive messages about herself or himself develops self-confidence and feels secure. Research suggests that children who are given non-verbal recognition in the form of positive physical contact develop physically, intellectually and emotionally more than those who are deprived of this kind of contact.

Positive non-verbal messages include:

- being hugged warmly
- being caressed
- being looked at when talked and/or listened to
- being held

The child who has a positive experience of the above and also of herself or himself in terms of the five physical senses – touching, seeing, hearing, smelling, tasting – will develop self-confidence and feelings of self-worth. As young children a lot of discoveries are made physically and if we are encouraged to enjoy our bodies we will develop a positive self-image.

Positive verbal messages include:

- 'I like you ...'
- 'You're great ...'
- 'I really enjoyed the way you ...'
- 'Thanks a lot, I really like it ...'

Positive verbal messages are empowering. They can be general or specific. If a child receives mostly positive verbal messages then she or he is encouraged to be herself or himself. The child develops feelings of self-worth and feels special. She or he learns not only to respect and value herself or himself but also to value and respect other people. The child believes in herself or himself. Such a child is able to develop her or his potential. Rather than being punished for doing something 'wrong' or 'differently' the child is encouraged to make sense of what she or he has done and to learn in a positive way from the experience.

EXERCISE: IDENTIFYING THE POSITIVE MESSAGES YOU RECEIVED AS A CHILD

What were the positive messages that you received from your parents and/or primary carers during your childhood?

Positive non-verbal messages:

Positive verbal messages:

What decisions about yourself and others do you remember making as a child as a result of the positive non-verbal and verbal messages that you received from your parents and/or primary carers?

Positive decisions about myself:

Positive decisions about others:

How do these positive decisions influence your attitude and behaviour now?

SUMMARY

Passive attitude and behaviour

Negative non-verbal and verbal messages from parents and/or primary carers – 'Don't ask questions', 'Do as you are told', 'Shut up!'

You think that it is best to keep quiet – 'Anything for a quiet life'.

You think that other people are better than you.

You lack the confidence to try things out for fear of being punished.

You imagine that people think you are no good at what you do.

You think that others are right and that you are in the wrong.

Manipulative attitude and behaviour

Negative non-verbal and verbal messages from parents and/or primary carers.

You feel helpless to change things.

You doubt yourself and mistrust others.

You imagine that others are wary of you, as you are of them.

You don't like yourself or other people very much.

Aggressive attitude and behaviour

Negative non-verbal and verbal messages from parents and/or primary carers.

You cover up your low self-esteem by appearing confident.

You make out that you don't need other people.

You try to be self-sufficient.

You compare yourself with others and put them down, so as to feel better about yourself.

You imagine that others don't see your lack of self-confidence.

Assertive attitude and behaviour

Positive non-verbal and verbal messages from parents and/or primary carers.

High self-esteem.

You feel equal to others.

You respect yourself and others.

THE NEXT STEP

Now that you have looked at some of the messages which you received as a child that have influenced your underlying attitudes about yourself and others, and your behaviour, you are ready to look at ways of developing a positive attitude and assertive behaviour.

Part II
Developing assertiveness in yourself

— *Step Four Developing assertiveness through positive self-recognition*

In this section you have an opportunity to look at:

- the kind of recognition which you give to yourself;
- how you can turn negative self-recognition into positive self-recognition.

SELF-RECOGNITION

Self-recognition refers to the kinds of thoughts you have about yourself and the kinds of feelings and body sensations that you experience. In any situation thoughts run through your mind; these thoughts may be accompanied by memories of yourself in previous, possibly similar situations. The memories may be of messages and decisions about yourself and others. Indeed you may actually visualize yourself in a previous situation and/or hear what was said to you or by you in that situation. The thoughts are also related to how you feel in your body. Particular body sensations are associated with particular thoughts and situations. How a person thinks and feels about herself or himself influences her or his behaviour, which in turn influences the behaviour of others.

Figure 1 shows how in any situation thoughts and feelings influence a person's behaviour.

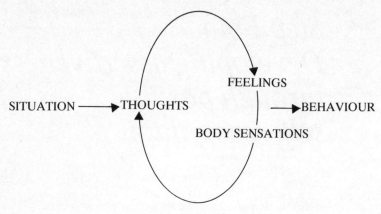

Figure 1

Negative self-recognition

When you are lacking in self-confidence your thoughts about yourself are negative and you feel uncomfortable and tense. Your behaviour, depending on your particular thoughts about yourself and others, will be passive, manipulative or aggressive. You are more likely to give to and receive from others negative recognition, which increases your negative thoughts and feelings about yourself and others.

Examples of negative self-recognition include:

- 'I'll never be any good as ...'
- 'I know I'm useless at managing others ...'
- 'They'll never agree to what I'm suggesting ...'
- 'I'm far too nervous to make this presentation ...'
- 'I know I'm stupid ...'
- 'I might as well give up now ...'

Negative thoughts such as these often lead to a person feeling uptight, resulting in headaches and low physical energy. Negative thoughts are characterized by being general and undermining of your self-worth. You will actually communicate what you are thinking and feeling non-verbally to others. Once you focus on the negative in yourself it is easy to spiral down, finding more and more not only in yourself but also in others that is negative (see

Figure 2). The exercise in this section gives you an opportunity to challenge some of our negative self-recognitions and turn them into positive recognitions leading to assertive behaviour.

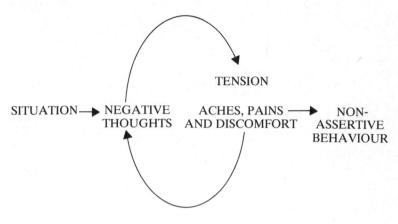

TENSION

SITUATION —► NEGATIVE   ACHES, PAINS —►   NON-
                THOUGHTS   AND DISCOMFORT   ASSERTIVE
                                                BEHAVIOUR

Figure 2

Positive self-recognition

When you feel self-confident your thoughts about yourself and others are positive, you feel relaxed and good in yourself. Your behaviour is assertive. You are more likely to give to and receive from others positive recognition which increases your thoughts and feelings of self-worth.

Examples of positive self-recognition include:

- 'I am good at making presentations'
- 'People will be interested in my views'
- 'I communicate my ideas clearly to others'
- 'I am confident in my abilities as a manager'

Positive self-recognition enhances your thoughts and feelings of self-worth. You may not always think or feel as positive as the above self-recognitions suggest, nevertheless when you are preparing for a situation in which you would otherwise behave non-assertively it is useful to think positively about yourself and others. When you enter into a situation with positive thoughts about yourself and others you will communicate to them that you are assertive. Once you start to look for the positive in yourself you will be surprised at how you are more able to find it not only in yourself but also in others (see Figure 3).

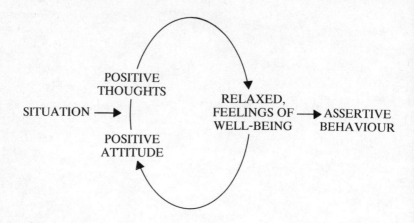

Figure 3

EXERCISE: TURNING NEGATIVE INTO POSITIVE SELF-RECOGNITION

Turning negative into positive self-recognition is the key to developing self-confidence and assertive behaviour. It is easier to decide to change your negative self-recognition than to actually do so in practice. The difficulty is due to your having got used to your negative thoughts, rather like a habit. Just as a habit is often difficult to give up, so too are the ways in which you have got used to thinking and feeling about yourself and others. My own view is that it is easier to give up something when you have something with which to replace it.

Negative self-recognition

Think about some of the situations in which you experience

yourself behaving non-assertively, in other words passive, manipulative or aggressive.

Write down some of the negative thoughts that you have about yourself in these situations:

What are some of the feelings and/or body sensations that you experience in these situations?

Positive self-recognition

Now think about yourself in these same situations and write down some positive thoughts which you could have about yourself that would help you to feel confident in yourself and to behave assertively. Write them in the present tense, and make sure that they are affirmative, for example, 'I am an effective manager', 'I am confident in my ability to motivate my subordinates'.

This list of positive self-recognitions is one to which you can keep adding as you develop more assertiveness. Some managers have found it useful to write their positive recognitions on a separate piece of paper which they then pin up to remind themselves to think positively.

What are some of the feelings and body sensations that you experience when feeling self-confident? You will find it useful to consciously remind yourself of how you feel when you are relaxed, particularly in situations in which you would otherwise feel uptight and tense.

SUMMARY

Passive attitude and behaviour
■ Negative self-recognition.
■ Negative thoughts about self as a person, 'I'm no good, other people know better than me'.
■ You put yourself down and invite others to do so.
■ You communicate your lack of self-esteem non-verbally to others.

You can develop assertiveness by:

1   challenging your negative thoughts about yourself;
2   turning your negative into positive recognition;
3   actively looking for the positive in yourself;
4   being specific about what you like in yourself;
5   being specific about what you can do well.

Manipulative attitude and behaviour
■ Negative self-recognition.
■ Negative thoughts about yourself and others, 'I know I'm no good, there's no hope for me, no one understands me round here'.
■ You put yourself down and put others down.
■ You communicate non-verbally to others your lack of self-esteem.

You can develop assertiveness by:

1   challenging your negative thoughts about yourself and others;
2   turning your negative into positive recognition;
3   actively looking for the positive in yourself and others;
4   being specific about what you like in yourself and others;
5   being specific about what you and others do well.

Aggressive attitude and behaviour
■ Negative self-recognition.
■ Negative thoughts about others, and indirectly yourself, 'People round here are a waste of time, if it wasn't for them I'd be alright'.
■ You put others down.
■ You try to communicate to others that you are confident but communicate non-verbally to others your lack of self-esteem.

You can develop assertiveness by:

1   challenging your negative thoughts about yourself and others;
2   turning your negative into positive self-recognition;
3   actively looking for the positive in others and yourself;
4   being specific about what you like in yourself and others;
5   being specific about what you and others do well.

Assertive attitude and behaviour

■ Positive self-recognition.
■ Positive thoughts about yourself and others, 'I am good at managing other people and the people with whom I work are a good team'.
■ You give positive recognition to others.
■ You communicate to others that you are confident through your non-verbal and verbal behaviour.

You can maintain assertiveness by:

1   monitoring your self-recognition and ensuring that it is positive;
2   adding to your list of positive self-recognitions.

MY KEY ACTION

> I can develop and maintain assertiveness by giving myself positive recognition for:

THE NEXT STEP

Now that you have looked at ways in which you develop assertiveness through positive self-recognition you are ready to look at how you can develop assertiveness through giving and receiving positive recognition.

Step Five
Developing assertiveness through giving and receiving positive recognition

In this section you have an opportunity to look at:

- the kind of recognition that you give to and receive from others;
- how you are going to get more positive recognition in order to develop your assertiveness.

RECOGNITION THAT YOU GIVE TO AND RECEIVE FROM OTHERS

There is a close relationship between self-recognition and the kind of recognition which you give to and receive from others. The more positive your thoughts and feelings about yourself and towards others the more likelihood there is that you will give to and receive from others positive recognition. There is a tendency for us to receive from others what we give to others in terms of the kind of recognition. The kind of recognition which you give to and receive from others varies according to your Life Position and your non-assertive attitude and behaviour.

Language is often a clue as to your thoughts and feelings about yourself and towards others. The person whose attitude and behaviour is non-assertive – in other words her or his attitude and behaviour is passive, manipulative or aggressive – tends not to take responsibility for how she or he feels and thinks but to blame others. By contrast, the person whose attitude and behaviour is assertive takes responsibility for how she or he thinks, feels and behaves.

The following case study illustrates very simply the difference between taking and abdicating responsibility for negative thoughts, feelings and behaviour.

Case study

Tom is the manager of an accounts department. He takes his job
--- riously and sets himself and others high standards. He is
:d by his colleagues in other departments for the speed at
e is able to supply them with the necessary information.
1siders himself to be the sort of person who works well
essure and likes to work with people who also work well
:ssure. He tends to feel irritated when others do not meet
ines he has set them or produce work which does not
tandards.

ember of his department appeared to be struggling to
idline and Tom was concerned that even if Steven made
e there would be mistakes to be corrected which would
er delay. Tom secretly thought that he should have
b himself and that way it would have been done, and
in the first place, by the deadline. When Steven did
iroduce the work, on the day of the deadline, Tom
noying that you are always at the last minute, Steven;
for me and the rest of the department. You make us
hat we're not going to meet the deadline – especially
.. ᴜᴄɪᴇ are mistakes to be corrected.'

Needless to say, Steven pointed out that he had made the deadline and that he thought Tom's remarks were unjust and he wanted to know who in the rest of the department was anxious about him meeting deadlines. An argument ensued, after which Tom felt extremely angry towards Steven and awkward about talking to him when they met later in the cafeteria.

Tom's immediate response to Steven was negative. He had been feeling anxious about Steven making the deadline and the possible extra work he himself would have to do correcting mistakes. When he spoke to Steven he did not take responsibility for how he had been feeling and added weight to his argument by saying that the rest of the department was also anxious about the deadline. The result was that he went away from the situation feeling even more negative than when he went into it. No doubt Steven also went away from the situation feeling negative and demotivated.

Tom's self-confidence was, he admitted, closely linked to what other people said about the department's performance. He was especially keen to maintain his reputation with regard to the department's speed of delivery. He felt that if they failed to keep on target then he personally would have failed and that he wouldn't be able to respect himself or be respected by others. His self-esteem was very dependent on others and not on inner self-recognition. This resulted in him blaming others when they fell short of his expectations in some way.

Tom's underlying Life Position was *I'm not OK – You're OK*; he had, however, learnt to cope with his lack of self-confidence by adopting the more aggressive Life Position *I'm OK – You're not OK*. This resulted in him neither giving to nor receiving positive recognition from others. He never asked for positive recognition from others, directly or indirectly, since he secretly feared that no one would be able to find anything positive to say to or about him.

Unfortunately, a lack of self-esteem tends to lead to further awkwardness, as it did in Tom's situation and more negative feelings and thoughts. On reflection, Tom felt that if he could develop his inner self-recognition then he would be able to express his anxiety and irritation in a way which left him, and the other person, feeling more positive and motivated. The key was to take responsibility for his feelings. In a similar situation in which he was taking responsibility for his attitude and behaviour he could say: 'Steven, thanks for meeting the deadline which I set. I have, however, been feeling anxious as the deadline neared and you hadn't finished the work. Indeed I feel extremely irritated when I think that you are not going to make it and that there are going to be mistakes which will need correcting. I think it may be useful in future, as the deadline nears, if we discuss what there is to be done and if I look through what you have done with you to check it – rather than wait until the deadline to do so. What do you think?'

Tom takes full responsibility for his thoughts and feelings; he also suggests a positive and creative way of dealing with them. In particular you will notice that Tom makes 'I' statements and draws on his own feelings and thoughts not on those of the department. Steven is also able to comment on the suggestion of Tom checking the work in progress with him and to make his own suggestions as to what would be useful for him. By both thanking Steven and giving him an opportunity to comment, Tom is giving him positive recognition, which in turn means that Steven responds by giving him positive recognition. Indeed, Steven welcomed the chance to discuss their working relationship, he also felt valued and appreciated for having met this particular deadline.

Everyone needs and wants to feel valued and appreciated; no one likes to feel that they are dispensable and easily replaceable. Nevertheless, many managers find it extremely difficult not only to give positive recognition to others, be they their peers, subordinates and/or bosses, but also to receive positive recognition from them, due to their own lack of self-confidence and positive self-recognition.

GIVING TO AND RECEIVING RECOGNITION FROM OTHERS

You can give to and receive recognition from others verbally and non-verbally. It can be about the person, in other words who she or he is irrespective of their behaviour, and/or it can be about their behaviour and performance.

Negative non-verbal recognition includes:

not looking at the person when she or he is talking;
ignoring the person.

Negative verbal recognition includes:

'That's a lousy piece of work you've done'
'There's no way you'll ever succeed doing it that way'
'You might as well give up now, before you make more of a mess'
'It's time we found someone to do a proper job instead of you'
'I know I should have done it myself'

Positive non-verbal recognition includes:

a warm handshake;
looking at the person when she or he is talking;
nodding in agreement with a person;
smiling in acknowledgement of the person.

Positive verbal recognition includes:

- 'Thanks, you've done a great job'
- 'Well done, I like it'
- 'Yes I think you're right'
- 'What do you think ...'
- 'I'd appreciate and value your comments'

When your self-esteem is low you give yourself negative self-recognition and invite others to give you negative recognition. For example, if you go into an interview situation thinking, 'I know I don't stand a chance of being promoted into the job, there are several people much better qualified than me ...', you are likely to feel extremely nervous and tense. Your behaviour will be non-assertive and the interviewers may well conclude that you are unsuitable for promotion. By contrast, when you enter an interview situation thinking, 'I know my experience and knowledge are suited to this job and I look forward to discussing the relevance of it to the job with the interviewers ...', whilst you may still feel some nervous apprehension your behaviour will be assertive. The interviewers are more likely to consider you for this promotion, and if not for this one, to remember you for a future promotion.

We often ask for the recognition which we receive indirectly, more than we ask for it directly, simply by our attitude and behaviour towards others which reflects the kind of recognition we give to ourselves. It is therefore important when developing assertiveness to become aware of negative attitudes and behaviour in order to change them into positive attitudes and behaviour.

Once you recognize the ways in which you directly and indirectly ask for the negative recognition that you receive, you can begin to look for ways of asking for positive recognition. When you consciously make an effort to give other people positive recognition you will receive it from them. As your self-esteem develops and your behaviour is more assertive you will be able to ask them directly for more positive recognition. For example, imagine one of your colleagues telling you how much she had enjoyed the meeting which you had chaired. Rather than shrugging off the positive recognition which she is giving you, you might consider asking her, 'What did I do that you thought worked especially well?'

EXERCISE: IDENTIFYING THE KINDS OF RECOGNITION YOU GIVE TO AND RECEIVE FROM OTHERS

You may find it useful to consider a typical day in your life at work, and the people with whom you interact most when completing this exercise. Consider the people you look forward to and enjoy interacting with and those who you tend to avoid.

What kind of recognition do you give to your peers? Give specific examples of non-verbal and verbal recognition:

What kind of recognition do you receive from your peers? Give specific examples of non-verbal and verbal recognition:

What kind of recognition do you give to your subordinates? Give specific examples of non-verbal and verbal recognition:

What kind of recognition do you receive from your subordinates? Give specific examples of non-verbal and verbal recognition:

What kind of recognition do you give to your boss or bosses? Give specific examples of non-verbal and verbal recognition:

What kind of recognition do you receive from your boss or bosses? Give specific examples of non-verbal and verbal recognition:

EXERCISE: LOOKING AT WHAT YOU CAN DO DIFFERENTLY SO AS TO GIVE AND RECEIVE MORE POSITIVE RECOGNITION TO AND FROM OTHERS

You may find it useful to think of people with whom you regularly interact and with whom you tend to exchange negative rather than positive recognition. For example, you may decide to focus on one or two relationships in which you tend to give and receive mostly negative recognition and in which you would like to change your behaviour so as to give and receive more positive recognition.

List some specific non-verbal and verbal kinds of positive recognition that you would like to give to others.

List some specific non-verbal and verbal kinds of positive recognition that you would like to receive from others.

What are you going to do in order to give and receive positive recognition? List some specific actions that you are going to take:

SUMMARY

Passive attitude and behaviour

Receives negative recognition from others in the form of put-downs.

Is often ignored in a group situation.

Tells others that she or he is no good and they tend to agree.

Gives others positive recognition from time to time, but is not convincing.

You can develop assertiveness by:

1   giving yourself more positive recognition;
2   recognizing that everyone is different and that you have strengths and limitations;
3   realizing that everyone is not better than you, that they too are different and have their strengths and limitations;
4   accepting positive recognition from others, not shrugging it off.

Manipulative attitude and behaviour

Focuses on the negative in self and others.

Rarely gives or receives positive recognition.

Gives negative recognition.

Mistrusts positive recognition from others and reads into it the negative.

You can develop assertiveness by:

1   actively focusing on the positive in yourself and others;
2   trusting the positive recognition you receive from others;
3   asking for positive recognition from others.

Aggressive attitude and behaviour

Keeps others at a distance so neither gives to nor receives from others positive recognition.

Tends to look for the negative in self and others.

Is very self-critical and critical of others.

Puts others down.

You can develop assertiveness by:

1   actively looking for the positive in yourself and others;
2   realizing that it is alright to make mistakes;
3   actively giving others positive recognition;
4   accepting positive recognition from others.

Assertive attitude and behaviour

■ Gives positive recognition to others.
■ Receives positive recognition from others.
■ Asks for positive recognition from others.
■ Recognizes that everyone has strengths and limitations.
■ Focuses on the positive in self and others.

You can maintain assertiveness by:

1   building on the positive in self and others;
2   giving more positive recognition to others;
3   asking others for specific positive recognition.

MY KEY ACTION

> I can develop and maintain assertiveness by giving and receiving the following kinds of positive recognition:

THE NEXT STEP

The focus has been on developing assertiveness through positive recognition, in other words positive thinking about yourself and others. The next step is to develop assertiveness by looking at ways of relaxing your body and of releasing tension.

Step Six
Developing assertiveness through relaxation

In this section you will discover how to use relaxation as one of the keys to:

■ developing self-confidence and behaving assertively;
■ maintaining self-confidence and assertive behaviour.

RELAXATION

Whilst positive self-recognition encourages you to think positively about yourself and others, relaxation exercises encourage you to feel fitter and healthier in yourself.

The simplest and easiest way of relaxing is to be aware of your breathing. When you are lacking in confidence you are more likely to hold your breath and to breathe shallowly. Holding your breath leads to tension in other parts of the body and to your not only feeling 'uptight' and 'on edge' but also to others perceiving you as 'uptight' and 'on edge'.

When you feel physically well you present yourself more assertively than when you feel physically unfit, tense and stressed. For more information and practical exercises on how to assess your vulnerability to stress, and how to develop strategies for thriving on stress read *Thriving on Stress* by Jane Cranwell-Ward.

One manager said that once he realized that his hands were tense most of the time, especially in situations in which he lacked self-confidence, by consciously relaxing them he felt more relaxed in himself and behaved much more assertively.

Another manager who previously had suffered from severe headaches whenever she had important meetings to attend found that by consciously using the breathing exercises she was able to relax and look forward to meetings without suffering from headaches.

Others perceive you very differently when your appearance and the image which you present is confident. Your appearance and the initial impression that you make can influence the outcome of a situation. If the first impression you make is one of lacking in self-confidence you will find it difficult to be assertive since people will respond to you as if you are non-assertive. You can use the relaxation exercises section as preparation for a potentially difficult situation and you can use them in the situation.

BREATHING RELAXATION

The breathing relaxation is easy to do in any situation and the body relaxation can be done as a quick body check or as a deeper relaxation.

EXERCISE: BREATHING RELAXATION

1 As you read now be aware of how you are breathing and the effect that this has on how you are sitting.

 • What, if any, parts of your body feel tense?

 • Is there a particular part of your body which you tense up when in a difficult or stressful situation?

2 Take a deep breath in and then as you breathe out do so with a sigh and let yourself relax. Sit in the chair so that the base of your back is firmly seated in the back of the chair and with your spine as straight as possible. Let the chair support you as you sit and make yourself comfortable so that there are no points of strain in your body.

3 Be aware of your shoulders and take another deep breath in and this time as you breathe out let your shoulders drop. You may be surprised at how you were previously holding your shoulders up and how far down they will go.

4   Repeat this process of breathing in and of consciously relaxing as you breathe out for a few minutes.

5   If you have identified a particular part of your body that you tense up, then focus on relaxing that part as you breathe out for a few minutes.

6   When you are ready, finish this breathing exercise by taking one deep breath in and out and look around the room.

   • How do you feel now?

   In particular notice any differences between how you felt before doing the breathing exercise and after completing it.

7   Whenever you feel yourself to be lacking in confidence and behaving non-assertively check out your breathing. Take a deep breath in and as you breathe out feel the old tension going out of your body and new energy coming in as you breathe in again.

BODY RELAXATION

The second relaxation encourages you to be aware of your breathing and to use it to help relax the whole of your body, starting with your feet. You can use it as a body check when you are feeling a lack of self-confidence and also as a deep relaxation. When you use it as a body check you can do each part of the exercise once sitting wherever you are. When you use it as a deep relaxation do each part of the exercise at least three times preferably with your eyes closed and lying down.

EXERCISE: BODY RELAXATION

1   Begin now by taking a few deep breaths in and out. As you breathe in take in new energy and as you breathe out release old tensions. Ensure that you are sitting comfortably and that your legs are uncrossed and your

feet firmly on the ground. Sit with a straight back with the base of your spine in the back of the chair.

2 Start by checking that your feet and legs are relaxed. Curl your toes up tightly and tighten the muscles of your legs as you breathe in and then as your breathe out release them. Do this a couple more times until you can feel the difference between feeling tense and relaxed in your feet and legs.

3 Next, as you breathe in hold the muscles of your stomach in tightly and then as you breathe out release them. Do this a couple more times until you can feel the difference for yourself between tension and relaxation in your stomach.

4 Check that your feet and legs are still relaxed, if not, tense and then relax them. Keep your breathing relaxed and comfortable.

5 Now clench your hands into tight fists as you breathe in and release them as you breathe out. You may like to shake both of your hands before tightening them again while breathing in and then releasing them on the next out breath.

6 On the next in breath lift your shoulders as far up to your ears as possible and hold them there before releasing and letting them drop on the next out breath. Do this a couple of times, especially if you suffer from headaches and/or back trouble.

7 Rotate your neck round slowly to the left three times and then slowly to the right three times. Then rotate your jaw to the left and then to the right a few times; don't be surprised if you hear some cracks as you release tension from this part of your body.

8 Then tighten the muscles in your face as you breathe in and as you breathe out release all the tension from your jaw and face.

9 Finally, remembering to keep your breathing relaxed and comfortable check that all parts of your body are relaxed, if not tighten that part while breathing in and release it on an out breath.

> 10 Open your eyes and look around the room. Take a deep breath in and then out. Stand up, and if it feels right to you simply shake your feet and your hands.

SUMMARY

Passive attitude and behaviour

Holds tension in the body, often in shoulders, neck and hands.
Looks ill at ease to others due to fidgeting, nail-biting.
Voice tends to get quieter and quieter until it is inaudible.
Shallow breathing resulting in high-pitched tone of voice.

You can develop assertiveness by:

1 consciously relaxing parts of the body which you tense up;
2 focusing on your breathing, and breathing more deeply in and out;
3 standing up straight with shoulders relaxed and chest open;
4 breathing deeply and carrying your voice through to the end of what you have to say.

Manipulative attitude and behaviour

Holds a lot of tension in the body.
Prone to aches and pains; headaches, backaches and to catch colds.
Appears to others as agitated.
Shallow breathing.
Speaks in monotone voice, lacking energy and vitality.

You can develop assertiveness by:

1 consciously focusing on your breathing, and breathing positive energy in and negative energy out;
2 consciously relaxing parts of the body in which you hold tension;
3 putting energy into what you have to say and expressing yourself using gestures.

Aggressive attitude and behaviour

- Holds tension in the body, often in the jaw and hands – both clenched.
- Holds tension in the knees and legs.
- Prone to headaches, neckache and backache.
- Voice often sounds tight due to shallow breathing.
- Talks fast and loud due to nervousness, gasps for breath.
- Sounds irritated to others.

You can develop assertiveness by:

1 consciously relaxing parts of the body which you tense up;
2 consciously focusing on your breathing, and breathing in and out more deeply;
3 regularly rotating your jaw and neck, in order to release tension;
4 breathing deeply, especially when you feel yourself becoming irritated.

Assertive attitude and behaviour

- Is aware of breathing.
- Able to relax parts of the body.
- Appears physically relaxed to others and calm.
- Expresses self freely using gestures.
- Has a lot of energy.
- Physically fit and well.
- Can switch off from work and relax.

You can maintain assertiveness by:

1 continuing to focus on your breathing;
2 breathing in positive energy and breathing out negative tensions;
3 relaxing parts of your body.

MY KEY ACTION

> I can develop and maintain assertiveness by consciously relaxing the following parts of my body:

THE NEXT STEP

You have looked at ways in which you can develop assertiveness through positive recognition of yourself and others, and through relaxation. The next step is to look at developing assertiveness through positive visualization. This involves visualizing yourself both thinking positively about yourself and others and being relaxed in certain situations.

Step Seven
Developing assertiveness through positive visualization

In this section you will discover how to use positive visualization as:

- an effective way of developing self-confidence and assertive behaviour;
- a way of preparing yourself for potentially difficult situations.

POSITIVE VISUALIZATION

When you lack self-confidence you tend to imagine and visualize yourself behaving passively, manipulatively or aggressively. You enter into a situation with a view of yourself and others which you then set up and live out.

Once you are aware of the negative images you can decide to change them into positive images of yourself and others. You can prepare for a potentially difficult situation by imagining yourself feeling confident and visualizing yourself behaving assertively.

Focusing on what you want to contribute and get out of a situation is part of effective communication. Preparing in advance by being clear as to your goals and then visualizing yourself being confident and asserting what you want, whilst respecting others, can make all the difference as to your behaviour in the actual situation.

Many managers behave non-assertively in a difficult situation, not only because they are lacking in confidence but also due to being ill-prepared. Indeed, a lot of time can be wasted at meetings by managers who are defending their positions, by behaving aggressively or passively, as a consequence of poor preparation and a lack of focusing on clear goals.

One of the difficulties managers have experienced with positive visualization is imagining and picturing the people with whom they are interacting responding positively. It is one thing to imagine yourself behaving assertively and quite another to imagine others behaving differently. Whilst this is true, managers have also reported their surprise when, as a result of positive visualization, they have experienced their previously hostile colleagues as behaving differently towards them.

You can use positive visualization as part of developing your self-confidence and as part of your preparation for going into what otherwise could be a non-assertive situation for you. Once you have experienced the positive results of preparing in this way you will readily be able to use it prior to any potentially difficult situation.

EXERCISE: DEVELOPING POSITIVE VISUALIZATION

Part one

Think of a recent situation in which you lacked self-confidence and behaved non-assertively. Make a note of the situation and how you picture yourself in it.

The following checklist of questions will help you to picture yourself in the situation:

1   How would you describe your behaviour?
      Passive
      Manipulative
      Aggressive

2   What are the particular characteristics of your non-verbal behaviour?

      a   If sitting, how are you sitting?
            Legs crossed
            Arms folded
            Body turned away or towards the other person, or people

b   If standing, how are you standing?
    Arms folded
    Hands in pockets
    One foot on the ground and the other wrapped
    round your standing leg

c   What are you doing with your hands?
    Clenched
    Fiddling with a pen
    Biting your nails
    Drumming your fingers
    Doodling

d   Eye contact
    Are you making eye contact?
    Are you avoiding eye contact?
    Do you look at the people you are talking to?
    Do you look at the other people when they are
    talking?

e   Tone of voice
    Is the tone of your voice raised?
    Are you speaking in a monotone?
    If you are talking to more than one person can
    they all hear you?

f   Breathing
    Notice the level of your breathing, is it shallow
    or deep?
    How tense are you?

3   What are your negative thoughts about yourself and
    others?

Part two

Now imagine yourself in the same situation with a clear
picture of yourself behaving assertively. Remember as part
of your preparation for the situation you need not only to
visualize yourself behaving assertively but also to have
clearly in focus your desired outcome. The following
checklist will help you prepare for and visualize yourself
behaving assertively in the situation

1 What is your goal in this situation?
   Is your goal clear?
   Is it specific?
   Is it realistic?

2 What are the characteristics of your non-verbal behaviour?
   a   If sitting, are you sitting with an open body posture?
   b   If standing, are you standing with both feet on the ground?
   c   Are your hands relaxed?
   d   Are you making eye contact?
   e   Does your tone of voice reflect what you are saying?
   f   Is your breathing relaxed and deep?

3 What positive thoughts do you have about yourself and others?

Run this picture of yourself feeling self-confident and behaving assertively through your mind several times. If your mind wanders or negative thoughts and images enter your mind, focus on your breathing and also on positive thoughts about yourself and others.

SUMMARY

Passive attitude and behaviour
- Negative visualization of not getting what you want.
- Visualizing others getting what they want.
- Picture yourself being undermined by others.
- Unclear goals.

You can develop assertiveness by:

1   positively visualizing yourself getting what you want;
2   visualizing yourself negotiating with others;
3   picturing yourself being listened to by others;

4   picturing yourself thinking and feeling positive;
5   visualizing yourself looking and feeling relaxed;
6   picturing others responding to you positively and assertively;
7   being clear about your goals.

Manipulative attitude and behaviour

■ Negative visualization.
■ Imagines the worst possible outcome to a situation.
■ Pictures self blocking others and being blocked by them.

You can develop assertiveness by:

1   visualizing others as being with you rather than against you;
2   picturing yourself and others working together to achieve desired outcomes;
3   thinking and feeling positive about yourself and others;
4   picturing yourself listening to others and what they are saying rather than imagining what their ulterior motives might be;
5   setting positive clear goals.

Aggressive attitude and behaviour

■ Negative visualization of self.
■ Picture self competing with others.
■ Imagine that in order to get what you want it means others not getting what they want.
■ Not open to negotiation on goals.
■ Feel threatened by others, so strongly defend what you want.

You can develop assertiveness by:

1   picturing yourself agreeing with others;
2   visualizing yourself seeing things from others' point of view;
3   recognizing that people are not necessarily against you when they disagree with you.

Assertive attitude and behaviour

■ Positive visualization.
■ Imagines self negotiating with others.
■ Pictures self working things out with others to achieve joint goals.

You can maintain assertiveness by:

1   focusing on the positive in yourself and others;
2   picturing yourself collaborating with others;
3   visualizing yourself listening to others' views;
4   picturing yourself responding positively to others' views which are different from your own.

MY KEY ACTION

I can develop and maintain assertiveness by visualizing myself:

THE NEXT STEP

You have looked at ways of developing assertiveness through positive recognition, relaxation and visualization. The next step is to learn the skills of communicating assertively irrespective of your Life Position and type of non-assertive behaviour. Whether you diagnosed your attitude and behaviour as passive, manipulative or aggressive you will find that through using the skills of communicating assertively that you not only develop and maintain assertive behaviour but also influence others to behave assertively towards you.

Step Eight
Developing assertiveness through using the appropriate communication skills

In this section you have an opportunity to look at the following communication skills which will help you to develop assertive behaviour:

- listening
- clarifying
- checking out assumptions
- open and closed questioning
- 'I' statements
- differentiating between what you think and feel, know and imagine
- positive talking
- talking the same language
- mirroring non-verbal behaviour

Successful use of all these communication skills depends on you listening to others and hearing what they are saying to you. This involves listening not only to what they are saying in terms of the words they are using to express themselves, and in particular key words, but also to how they are expressing themselves.

LISTENING

Listening to people involves paying attention to how they are expressing what they are saying, in other words being aware of the non-verbal behaviour and the verbal language. In particular, listen to their tone of voice and the emphasis that they place on words, this will help you to understand what is of real importance to them.

You can communicate to others that you are listening to them non-verbally by looking at them when they are talking, and nodding to show that you have heard what they are saying. All too often people do not look at the person who is talking, for example in meetings, and miss vital clues as to what they are really saying. You can communicate to people that you are listening using a variety of other skills, including clarifying, checking out assumptions and questioning, which are described under separate headings below.

On occasions you are likely to notice that there are incongruities between what the person is saying and how she or he is expressing it, in other words between the verbal and the non-verbal behaviour. For example, a person may reassure you that everything is absolutely alright but do so in a monotone and lack-lustre tone of voice. When you are busy and under pressure what you want to hear is that everything is alright and you may not notice or you may try to overlook the incongruities in a hope that everything is alright.

Reflecting back to people the key words which they are using communicates to them that you are listening. It can encourage someone to elaborate further and can also be a useful way of inviting people to clarify what they are saying.

Key words are those which the person emphasizes, for example, with a gesture and a change in the tone of voice. They may also be words which the person repeats severally, albeit in different ways.

People will often deny how they are feeling about a situation verbally; however, if you listen to them carefully you will hear in the tone of voice their true feelings. For example, you may have had occasion to feedback to someone your observations of their aggressive behaviour only to have her or him strongly deny such behaviour. It may be that you have genuinely made a mistake in your perception of her or his behaviour; on the other hand the strength of her or his denial may be telling you that indeed they are angry about the situation.

EXERCISE: IMPROVING YOUR LISTENING SKILLS

How do you rate your listening skills? The following questions are designed to help you think about your listening skills and to decide if and what you need to do to improve them.

1   Do you consider yourself to be someone who listens and pays attention to both what people are saying and how they are expressing it?

2   Do you tend to finish off people's sentences for them or allow them to finish what they are saying?

3   Do you have a tendency to interpret and 'talk over' other people when they are talking?

4   Do you look at people when you are talking to them?

5   Do you look at people when they are talking to you?

6   Do you reflect back to people the key words that they use?

Improving my listening skills

What I need to do less of in order to improve my listening skills:

What I need to do more of in order to improve my listening skills:

CLARIFYING

Clarifying is especially useful in a situation where there is a misunderstanding between you and another person and/or where you have not understood what the person is really trying to say. When you are unclear about something – for example, the key point of a discussion or the objectives of a meeting – the chances are that you are not on your own. By your seeking clarification you will be helping not only the person who is talking but also others who are likewise confused or unclear. Clarifying what the person is saying early on in a discussion can save a lot of time and a lot of misunderstandings. For example:

- 'So what you are saying is . . .'.
- 'Am I right in thinking that your feeling is that we should . . .'.
- 'Before we go on I'd like to check my understanding of what you are saying . . .'.

EXERCISE: USING CLARIFICATION

When you are in a situation in which you are unclear as to what is being said do you seek clarification?

In a meeting, for example, if you were unclear as to the objectives would you seek clarification or would you hope to some how pick them up as the meeting progressed?

When you do not understand what is being said do you say so?

I need to seek more clarification particularly in the following situations:

CHECKING OUT ASSUMPTIONS

When you are under pressure and/or preoccupied with other things you are more likely to make assumptions about people and what they are saying in a vain hope to save time. The tendency to make assumptions and to jump to conclusions about people and what they are saying is one which leads to many non-assertive interactions between people. This is especially true of people in meetings. Managers have often said how surprised they have been when they have taken the time to check out their assumptions and listen to a colleague with whom they have previously had difficulties communicating.

EXERCISE: CHECKING OUT ASSUMPTIONS

Do you tend to make assumptions about people and what they are saying?

Do you tend to leap to conclusions about people and what they are saying?

I need to check out the following assumptions that I have made about:

OPEN AND CLOSED QUESTIONING

Effective questioning of others depends on your listening to them carefully. Questioning can be part of the process of clarifying what people are saying and of checking out any assumptions which you have made about them and what they are saying. It can also be a useful way of opening up communication between you and others, providing your questions are open and invite a response from them. When you are busy and eager to get on with other tasks you may tend to ask questions which are closed rather than open-ended.

Closed questions are useful when you are seeking specific information and when you and the other person understand that this is the context in which they are being asked. Otherwise closed questions lead to stilted communication and often to either passive and/or aggressive behaviour.

Open questions are those which begin with 'What ...', 'How ...', 'Which ...', 'When ...', 'Who ...' and 'Why ...', for example:

- 'What do you think would be the best course of action for us to take?'
- 'How do you think we should go about it?'
- 'Which of the alternatives do you think would be the most effective?'
- 'When do you think would be the right time to commence the project?'
- 'Who do you think would be the best person to head up the project?'
- 'Why do you think we should consider that particular person?'

EXERCISE: USING OPEN AND CLOSED QUESTIONS

Do you ask open questions of others in order to find out how they are feeling and what they are thinking about topics or issues under discussion?

I need to ask more open questions especially in the following situations and/or of the following people:

'I' STATEMENTS

The person whose behaviour is assertive recognizes that she or he is responsible, not other people, for her or his actions. The way in which you use the spoken language communicates to others whether or not you believe yourself to be responsible for your actions.

When you lack self-confidence you are less likely to express yourself to others clearly and directly. When you are confident in yourself you are more able to take responsibility for your feelings and thoughts and to express them in a way which encourages others to respond directly to you.

One of the easiest and simplest ways of taking responsibility for yourself is to use 'I' statements. For example, when you wish to put forward a suggestion it is much more effective to begin by saying

'I'd like to suggest that we ...', instead of 'Don't you think that ...?'

EXERCISE: USING 'I' STATEMENTS

> When you say what you think do you tend to say 'you', 'one' or 'we' rather than 'I'?
>
> I need to take more responsibility for myself, especially in the following situations:

DIFFERENTIATING BETWEEN WHAT YOU THINK AND FEEL, KNOW AND IMAGINE

It is useful to differentiate between what you think and feel, know and imagine about and/or in a situation. There is a vast difference between telling people 'I know that you will all agree with me ...' and 'I imagine that you will probably all agree with me ...'. People are likely to be far more responsive to you when you give them the opportunity to assert themselves rather than making an incorrect assumption.

Expressing how you feel about something or towards someone is much easier to do when you recognize that the feelings you are experiencing are yours. Very often people will say that they think something rather than being clear that this is how they are feeling.

The person who denies responsibility for their feelings and/or for having feelings at all, is more likely to say, 'You make me feel very frustrated ...' and/or 'You're making me feel very upset by what you are saying ...'. When you assert your feelings and take responsibility for them you enable others to express and take responsibility for their feelings; for example, 'I'm feeling very uncomfortable about what you have just said ...' or 'I am feeling angry about the way in which things have ...'.

It is worth remembering that in exactly the same situation someone else will feel totally differently. Thus you may be feeling angry and frustrated about something about which someone else feels upset and sad. This is particularly useful to remember when you experience yourself projecting onto someone else how you would feel in her or his situation.

In many situations the use of intuition and imagination will be extremely valuable. It is, however, important to acknowledge that what you are saying – be it a thought or a feeling – is based on an intuition. All too often people deny their intuition or make out that what they think is indeed a fact and something that they have carefully thought through; when indeed an intuition is often a spontaneous response to a situation. Rather than stating, 'I know that there is a difficulty about who works on this project ...' it is more assertive to say, 'My hunch is that there is some difficulty about who will be working on this project ...'.

EXERCISE: DIFFERENTIATING BETWEEN WHAT YOU THINK AND FEEL, KNOW AND IMAGINE

How well do you differentiate between what you think and feel, know and imagine?

Do you tend to make ideas sound like facts by saying 'I know ...'?

Do you say 'I think ...' when really it is a feeling?

Do you say 'I imagine' and/or 'I have a hunch that ...'

I need to differentiate more between:

POSITIVE TALKING

Just as self-recognition in the form of positive statements about yourself is a key to developing self-confidence and assertiveness, so too is talking to others positively. Positive talking involves using positive and affirmative words rather than negatives.

All too often managers communicate using negative words; for example, the manager who says to a colleague, 'Don't worry, there's no problem really, everything's under control' is, by the very use of the words 'worry' and 'problem' suggesting to the colleague that there is a problem to worry about. Indeed the colleague may not have been conscious of there being a problem nor was she worrying; however, now she will worry unconsciously if not consciously.

Positive talking is not about denying that there are problems but it is about talking about them in a non-problem way. For example, the manager could have asserted to his colleague, 'We have had some difficulties, however, I am confident that we have now got them under control.' The use of the word 'confident' reassures his colleague that although there have been difficulties they are now under control.

The manager who puts an idea forward at a meeting by saying, 'I've had an idea which I feel confident will work ...' is far more likely to meet with a positive and assertive response from her colleagues than the manager who begins by saying, 'I don't know if this will work but I think it might if we try ...'.

Likewise, the manager whose behaviour is assertive is more ready to consider alternative solutions to problems. Instead of saying 'Yes, but ...' which tends to preface a negative comment, the manager says 'Yes, and ...' which encourages open discussion. This simple switch from 'but' to 'and' can encourage creative thinking and positive talking.

Another equally straightforward way of encouraging positive talking is, instead of talking about things in 'either/or' terms, to talk about them in terms of 'as well as ...'.

Thus being aware of the language that you use and your non-verbal behaviour is a key to successful self-assertion. When you assert yourself using language which is positive and non-verbal behaviour which is congruent with what you are saying you will have a much greater impact on others and influence them to respond assertively to you.

EXERCISE: USING POSITIVE TALKING

How positive is your talking?

When you are talking with your colleagues do you use language which is negative, leading to negative thinking and talking, or do you use positive language which encourages creative thinking and positive talking?

I need to be more creative in my thinking and positive talking in the following situations and with the following people:

TALKING THE SAME LANGUAGE

The skill of reflecting back to people what they have said is particularly useful in that it lets them know that you are listening and have heard what they are saying to you. The skill requires paying attention to the language of the other person. The language that a person uses tells you how she or he processes information in terms of the five senses:

- visual (see)
- auditory (hear)
- kinesthetic (feel)
- gustatory (taste)
- olfactory (smell)

The senses which most people use are visual, auditory and kinesthetic. Most people use a combination of visual, auditory and kinesthetic sense-making processes but have one which they prefer to use. Careful listening to others will tell you which of these three is their preferred process.

The list of phrases and words below will help you to recognize not only your own preferred process but also those of others. Once you are readily able to recognize your own and others' processes you will be able to consciously reflect back to others their process and thus facilitate communication between you and them. Frequently misunderstandings arise due to people simply not recognizing that they process information differently. Reflecting back to people using their preferred process means that you are literally speaking to their language.

Checklist: Visual sense-making process

A person whose preferred sense-making process is visual is likely to communicate her or his experience using the following:

Phrases

1   'I see what you mean ...'
2   'I get the picture ...'
3   'I imagine that you ...'

Words

- vision
- image
- clarify
- idea
- demonstrate
- obvious
- focus
- illusion
- look
- preview
- expose
- insight

- perception
- clear
- picture
- notice
- bright
- vague
- show
- hazy
- glimpse
- colourful
- perspective

Checklist: Auditory sense-making process

A person whose preferred sense-making process is auditory is likely to communicate her or his experience using the following:

Phrases

1   'I hear what you say ...'
2   'A balance between the two is ...'
3   'Harmony is important to me ...'

Words

listen	■ interview
talk	■ remark
noisy	■ inquire
discuss	■ articulate
call	■ announce
loud	■ communicate
told	■ pronounce
shout	■ ask
audible	■ recall
harmonize	■ utter

Checklist: Kinesthetic sense-making process

A person whose preferred sense-making process is kinesthetic is likely to communicate her or his experience using the following:

Phrases

1   'I feel that what you're getting at is ...'
2   'I sense that you're feeling uncomfortable with the decision ...'
3   'I do understand how you feel ...'

Words

touch	■ unbearable
■ pressure	■ tension
hurt	■ warm
tense	■ sensitive
relaxed	■ soft
concrete	■ handle
irritated	■ grasp
firm	■ active
stress	■ motion

EXERCISE: IDENTIFYING YOUR PRIMARY PROCESS

1   Which of the three lists contains words which you
    use to express yourself most of the time?
    Visual
    Auditory
    Kinesthetic

2   Which of the three lists contains words which you use to
    express yourself some of the time?
    Visual
    Auditory
    Kinesthetic

3   Which of the three lists contains words which you rarely
    use to express yourself?
    Visual
    Auditory
    Kinesthetic

I need to pay particular attention to people who have the
following sense-making process and which is the one I least
use:

MATCHING SENSE-MAKING PROCESSES

The skill of matching involves using the same sense-making
process as the person with whom you are communicating. It
depends on a combination of listening to the other person, recognizing her or his preferred process and then communicating with
her or him using the same kind of language. It doesn't mean that
you use the same words and phrases, rather that you use the
language of her or his preferred process.

Many managers are surprised when they realize that some of
their difficulties in communicating assertively with others have
been due to their speaking a 'different language'. Whilst it is relat-
ively straightforward to match when the person has the same
sense-making process as yourself it requires more effort to match
the person who has a different sense-making process to yourself.

You will be better able to communicate to and influence others
if you are aware of and match their sense-making processes.

EXERCISE: MATCHING SENSE-MAKING PROCESSES

> Pay attention to the colleagues with whom you interact
> closely and identify their primary and secondary
> sense-making processes:
>
> Name: Primary process:
>   Secondary process:
>
> Name: Primary process:
>   Secondary process:
>
> Name: Primary process:
>   Secondary process:

MIRRORING NON-VERBAL BEHAVIOUR

In addition to using the language of a person's preferred sense-making process and key words in order to communicate effectively you can mirror her or his non-verbal behaviour. Mirroring others' non-verbal behaviour is something that we all do unconsciously. However, becoming conscious of your non-verbal behaviour enables you to choose the behaviours that you want to mirror.

You can change your non-verbal behaviour in order to influence that of the other person. For example, she or he may be behaving aggressively towards you, pointing a finger at you and talking in a loud voice. Rather than mirroring the person's gestures and tone of voice you can consciously choose to relax, breathe deeply and talk in a calm manner. In this way you will influence the other person's behaviour, encouraging them to also behave assertively. She or he may still be feeling angry and frustrated but you are using your own behaviour to help the person express her or his feelings in a way which is assertive rather than aggressive.

SUMMARY CHECKLIST OF COMMUNICATION SKILLS

Listening

Listening and being aware of incongruities between verbal language and non-verbal behaviour. Reflecting back key words a person uses.

Clarifying

Understanding what the person is saying to you by seeking clarification. In a group situation seeking clarification will help clarify things for others.

Checking out assumptions

Check out that you do understand the other person in order to avoid misunderstandings and time-wasting.

Open and closed questioning

Use open questions to encourage the person to talk, open questions usually begin with 'What ...', 'Which ...', 'How ...', 'Why ...', 'When ...', 'Who ...'. Use closed questions to gather factual information and/or to get a 'Yes' or 'No' response.

'I' statements

Take responsibility for your attitude and behaviour by saying 'I' rather than 'you', 'one' or 'we'.

Differentiating between what you think and feel, know and imagine

Being clear as to whether what you are saying is a thought or a feeling; a fact or a hunch.

Positive talking

Talking to others in a positive and affirmative way, inspire confidence whilst still acknowledging difficulties.

Talking the same language

Listen to people's language in order to find out which sense-making process they use – visual (see), auditory (hear) kinesthetic (feel) – and use the same language to communicate that you are listening to and understanding them.

Matching sense-making processes

Use the same sense-making process as the people with whom you are talking in order to facilitate communication.

Mirroring non-verbal behaviour

Be aware of the other person's non-verbal behaviour and reflect the same and/or different behaviours depending on whether or not they are assertive. Influence the other person's behaviour using your own assertive non-verbal behaviour.

MY KEY ACTION

In order to develop and maintain assertiveness I need to practise the following communication skills:

THE NEXT STEP

You have diagnosed and analysed your attitude and behaviour. You have looked at ways of developing assertiveness through focusing on your attitude towards yourself through positive self-recognition, positive recognition of others, relaxation and visualization; and ways of developing assertive behaviour through the use of appropriate communication skills. The next step is to look at ways of developing and maintaining assertiveness in others.

Part III
Developing and maintaining assertiveness in others

Step Nine
Developing and
maintaining assertiveness
in others through
influencing their behaviour

In this section you have an opportunity to look at the ways in which:

■ having a positive attitude and behaving assertively towards people can influence them to behave assertively;
■ you can use your positive attitude and behaviour to influence a colleague with whom you work to develop her or his assertiveness.

INFLUENCING THE ATTITUDE AND BEHAVIOUR OF OTHERS BY HAVING A POSITIVE ATTITUDE AND BEHAVING ASSERTIVELY TOWARDS THEM

Influencing the attitude and behaviour of others through your own positive attitude and assertive behaviour towards them is one of the most powerful ways of helping people to develop assertiveness. The more positive and assertive your approach to people the more likely the response from them will be positive and assertive. The benefits of using your assertive behaviour to influence others, for example, in meetings and when making presentations, are that the people will be more receptive to your ideas and suggestions and will respond creatively to them.

Many managers have reported how very different the response is, to them and their ideas, when they themselves are feeling confident about themselves and their ideas. Likewise you may have noticed already that when you have a positive attitude of mind you are more assertive and receptive towards others. On those occasions when you have a negative attitude of mind your behaviour is non-assertive towards others and they in turn respond non-assertively to you.

One of the difficulties experienced by some managers is their inability to maintain their positive and assertive attitude, particularly during or after a stressful situation. What they tend to do is to literally carry over the negative attitude from one encounter into the next.

It is on these occasions that you can help yourself switch from a negative to positive attitude by giving yourself positive self-recognition. One of the dangers of not switching from a negative to positive attitude of mind is a downward spiralling effect. In other words, the more negative your attitude of mind the more non-assertive your behaviour and the more negative and non-assertive the response from others towards you. Being aware of your negative attitude and non-assertive behaviour gives you the opportunity to change and to influence the behaviour of others so that there is an upward spiralling effect.

When you are managing someone whose attitude is negative and whose behaviour is non-assertive it is important not to respond negatively and non-assertively but to use your own positive attitude and assertive behaviour to influence their attitude and behaviour.

When to use a positive attitude and assertive behaviour to influence the attitude and behaviour of others

The strategy of influencing others through having a positive attitude and behaving assertively is one which can be used to help people develop assertiveness in all situations. Irrespective of the person's underlying Life Position, negative attitude and non-assertive behaviour this strategy is a way of beginning to develop assertiveness in them.

For some people, however, their negative attitude and lack of self-confidence may be so great that you will need to use one of the other strategies to help them develop assertiveness.

Someone who has a negative attitude and whose behaviour is passive, manipulative or aggressive most of the time may have difficulty in responding to your positive attitude and assertive behaviour. The person may be so lacking in confidence and self-esteem that she or he is initially unable to respond in a different way. In this case you may need to help the person develop assertiveness by giving her or him some good quality feedback about her or his non-assertive behaviour and give examples to the person of what it means to have a positive attitude and behave assertively.

How to influence someone who has a negative attitude and passive behaviour

Once you have identified the person's attitude and behaviour to be negative and passive, respectively, you are in a position to help her or him develop a positive attitude and assertive behaviour. In particular, the people who have a negative attitude and passive behaviour need to be shown that they are valued. All too often they withdraw from discussions and draw back from taking on responsibility due to their lack of confidence. As a consequence they are often overlooked by others, which serves to confirm their negative attitude and non-assertive behaviour.

Listed below are some of the ways in which you can help them to develop a positive attitude and assertive behaviour:

1   Make a conscious effort to listen and look at them when they are talking.
2   Invite and encourage them to contribute to a discussion.
3   Thank them for their contributions, however small.
4   Give them responsibility initially for tasks which you know they can achieve.
5   Encourage them to ask for help when needed.

How to influence someone who has a negative attitude and manipulative behaviour

When you have identified a person's attitude and behaviour to be negative and manipulative, respectively, you are in a position to influence her or his behaviour to help the person develop assertiveness. The person who has a negative attitude and whose behaviour is manipulative is probably the most difficult and challenging to influence since she or he usually has very low-esteem and is lacking in confidence. Indeed, such a person is likely to be suspicious of you and your positive attitude and assertive behaviour. Nevertheless, you can influence the person albeit slowly and probably in small steps. People who have a negative attitude and manipulative behaviour often switch from behaving manipulatively to behaving either passively and/or aggressively before they develop a positive attitude and assertive behaviour. The challenge is not to give up on these people, who in some way have given up on themselves, but to persevere with them.

Listed below are some of the ways in which you can help them to develop a positive attitude and assertive behaviour:

1   Find things which you can entrust to the person.
2   Listen to the person and look at her or him.
3   Challenge the person without putting her or him down.
4   Make sure that you do not give up on the person by ignoring and/or discounting her or him.

How to influence someone who has a negative attitude and aggressive behaviour

When you have identified a person's attitude and behaviour as being negative and aggressive, respectively, you can influence her or him to develop assertiveness. People who have a negative attitude and whose behaviour is aggressive have low self-esteem and are lacking in self-confidence. They often give the impression of being confident but this is only a way of hiding their lack of confidence. They need just as much help in developing assertiveness as the people who have a negative attitude and whose behaviour is passive and/or manipulative. Underneath the hard exterior is a soft and often vulnerable person who is well-defended. Indeed their defences are usually so well-established that they are often unaware of when someone has a positive attitude towards them. Their assumption about themselves is that they have to fight to get what they want and to defend their position at all costs.

The challenge to you is to help them realize that they do not always have to be on the defensive, that people are not always out to get them and that you and they can both be right. In other words they can get what they want without undermining others.

Listed below are some of the ways in which you can help them develop a positive attitude and assertive behaviour:

1   Listen to the person; look at her or him when listening and when you are talking to her or him.
2   Look for points in the person's argument with which you agree.

3 Show them that you are working towards an *I win: You win* outcome.
4 Thank the person for her or his contribution.
5 Delegate to the person when appropriate and show her or him that responsibility and control can be shared.

BENEFITS TO YOU, THE OTHER PERSON AND YOUR WORKING RELATIONSHIP

You will notice that the more positive recognition that you give to people the more you will receive from them. In this way you will help others to develop their assertiveness and in particular you will maintain an openness between you and them. Indeed the more you begin to look for the positive in others the more you will find it in them.

People who feel appreciated for who they are and what they do are more motivated in their work. They get involved in and are more committed to one another and to the work; and they are more creative and productive.

CASE STUDY

In the following case study Mike is a manager in the Customer Support Centre of a large computer company. He deals with several of the company's major clients and is known by his colleagues as the 'trouble shooter'. Mike described his job as dealing with problems and complaints often from people who themselves are under pressure. Most of the time he enjoys a close working relationship with the clients; however, one particular client, after a series of recurring problems had not been solved by the division, announced on the phone to Mike that his company would be taking its business to an independent computer support service.

At the time Mike was taken unawares by the client's outburst since John, one of his team, had been dealing with the company. However, he arranged to meet the client the next day and reassured him that the problems would be solved within the week. The client agreed that, providing they were solved by the end of the week, he would not take the business elsewhere.

Mike understandably felt angry. He was angry with himself for not having been aware of the problems not being solved; and for having allowed the situation to get to the point at which the client was now threatening to take the business to another company. His immediate reaction was to call John into the office and tell him just how he felt and what he thought about him.

Mike was aware that under threat and pressure his behaviour was aggressive. In this situation he felt blamed and was all set to blame John. A typical example of what happens when someone 'passes the buck'. Mike knew that in order to find out and understand what had been going on between John and the client he was going to have to change his own behaviour from aggressive to assertive. In other words he would first have to take responsibility for not monitoring John's work. Then he would have to listen to and talk with John about what they could do to solve the problems immediately.

Identifying the person's negative attitude and non-assertive behaviour

Mike began the meeting by saying that by the end of it he wanted to be clear about how he and John, together, could solve their problems with the customer and how in future he could best help John to deal with this sort of situation so that it didn't happen again. Notice that Mike refers to 'their problems' rather than 'your problems'. In this way he is stating to John that the responsibility for solving the problems is shared by both of them. He then apologized to John for not having been more involved in his work.

John told Mike that when he called him into the office he knew it would be to talk about the client with whom he had been experiencing tremendous difficulty. John said that he had felt unable to talk to Mike about the growing problems, fearing that Mike would think him incompetent and at worst that he would lose his job. He had been hoping that, somehow, the problems would sort themselves out. He was therefore surprised when, instead of being shouted down and harangued for his incompetency, Mike began by apologizing for his lack of involvement in John's work.

Mike diagnosed that John's Life Position was *I'm not OK – You're OK*; and that it was John's underlying lack of self-confidence that had made it difficult for him to talk with Mike about his growing problems with this particular customer. He realized that John's attitude was negative and that his behaviour was passive in that he had been hoping the problem would somehow solve itself rather than getting on with solving it.

Mike checked his diagnosis of John's behaviour against his own behaviour. His initial reaction, you will remember, had been to shout at and blame John for his total incompetence. This kind of aggressive response is frequently elicited by people whose behaviour is passive. Mike realized that by behaving aggressively towards John he would simply be reinforcing John's negative attitude about himself and his passive behaviour. He knew that under threat John would comply with whatever he told him to do but that in the long term he would neither get commitment from John nor get him to take on more responsibility.

Strategy: Influencing the person's behaviour

In this situation Mike decided that the best way to help John develop self-confidence and assertive behaviour was to behave assertively and to work closely with him in solving the problems. He was committed to helping John develop assertive behaviour since he firmly believed in people being responsible for themselves and their work. Indeed, it was this very belief that had resulted in him not getting involved in John's work. What he had not realized was that John needed much more support and encouragement from him.

By being open and honest with John at the outset of the meeting Mike not only surprised John but also helped him to be assertive. Mike listened carefully to John's difficulties with the customer. John was relieved to have the opportunity to discuss them with Mike. Up until then he had imagined that everyone was managing their work with no trouble and he had pretended to be keeping up with his work so as 'not to let the side down'.

Mike questioned John in order to fully understand the situation and how it had developed. He asked John how he thought he could have managed it differently and what he thought would be the best course of action in terms of solving the problems for the customer. In this way Mike encouraged John to take some responsibility for sorting out the problem.

Thus Mike's strategy was to use his own assertive behaviour to influence John's behaviour. In this way he encouraged John to take responsibility for his own behaviour and to acknowledge the problems with the customer. By the end of the meeting John felt more motivated and committed not only to deal with the present difficult situation with the customer but also to deal with problems as and when they arose rather than hoping that they would somehow resolve themselves.

Regular reviewing

Mike realized that this was only the start of helping John to develop self-confidence and assertive behaviour and that he would need to give him positive feedback about his behaviour whenever possible. His first opportunity came the following day when he and John visited the customer. Previously John would have abdicated responsibility and declined going with Mike to the meeting; however, it was he who suggested that he attend the meeting for which he prepared and as a result established credibility with the customer, and with this renewed commitment to and enthusiasm for his work saw to it personally that the computer problems were solved by the end of the week.

Benefits to Mike, John and their working relationship

Mike felt, on the strength of this experience, that he could delegate more to John. John welcomed the increased responsibilities and the more regular feedback from Mike. Their working relationship was far more relaxed and they regularly sought each other out to discuss ideas.

EXERCISE: DEVELOPING ASSERTIVENESS IN OTHERS THROUGH INFLUENCING

> 1   Select a person who you think and feel you could develop assertiveness in through influencing her or him by having a positive attitude and behaving assertively towards the person. The person may be a colleague whom you have already identified as having a negative attitude and non-assertive behaviour. Who is the person and what is her or his typical negative attitude and non-assertive behaviour and/or combination of non-assertive behaviours:

Passive?
Manipulative?
Aggressive?

2   Think of a recurring situation in which you encounter
the person and experience her or him as having a
negative attitude and behaving non-assertively. In
terms of your own behaviour towards the person
what could you do differently towards her or him in
order to develop her or his assertiveness? Be as
specific as possible, giving examples of what you
could say to the person by way of positive
recognition. For example, you may decide to thank
the person face-to-face for a piece of work rather
than taking it for granted that she or he would do it.
Alternatively you may have a tendency not to
look at the person when asking her or him to do a
piece of work and you may decide to look at the
person as a way of giving her or him positive
recognition non-verbally.

3   How do you imagine that the person will respond
differently and assertively towards you? In other
words how will you know that your positive attitude
and assertive behaviour are helping the person to
develop assertiveness?

MY KEY ACTION

> In order to develop and maintain assertiveness in others
> through using my own positive attitude and assertive
> behaviour to influence them, I need to:

THE NEXT STEP

The next step is about helping people to develop assertiveness through giving them good quality feedback, and encouraging them to give you good-quality feedback. The giving and receiving of good-quality feedback can be part of using your own positive attitude and assertive behaviour to influence others and develop assertiveness in them.

Step Ten
Developing and maintaining assertiveness in others through the giving and receiving of good quality feedback

In this section you have an opportunity to look at:

■ The ways in which you can give good quality feedback to others about their behaviour in order to help them develop and maintain assertiveness. There is a checklist: 'Giving good quality feedback to others'.

■ What you need to do in order to receive good quality feedback from others in order to develop and maintain assertive relationships. There is a checklist: 'Receiving good quality feedback from others'.

■ The importance of regular reviewing, in terms of giving to and receiving feedback from each other regularly.

■ A case study illustrating the effective use of developing assertiveness in another person and an assertive working relationship.

■ An exercise for you to complete on giving and receiving good-quality feedback.

GIVING GOOD QUALITY FEEDBACK

As a manager, giving feedback to people about their behaviour is an integral part of managing and helping others to be assertive and creative in themselves and in their work. Giving open and honest feedback to people is part of respecting them for who they are and what they do. When you give feedback from an *I'm OK – You're*

OK Life Position on a regular basis you will find that the person respects you for the feedback.

Good quality feedback is about giving positive feedback as well as constructive feedback to people. It is not about being nice to people, indeed it can mean that you have to be critical of their behaviour. The key to giving good quality feedback is the spirit in which you give it to people. In other words if you respect them and genuinely think that the person can benefit from the feedback then you will give the feedback to them in a way which is developing of their self-confidence and self-esteem.

Do give positive feedback when the person behaves assertively. Remember that the most effective way of influencing others is through recognizing and appreciating them for their assertive behaviour. All too often people get recognition for their non-assertive behaviour, which simply serves to reinforce their negative attitude and non-assertive behaviour.

The following checklist on giving feedback applies not only to helping someone to develop self-confidence and assertive behaviour but also to giving feedback in any situation.

Checklist: Giving good quality feedback

1 Check that your motives for giving feedback are about helping the person to change her or his behaviour from non-assertive to assertive.
2 Ensure that your attitude is positive and your behaviour assertive.
3 Give the feedback at the time if possible, otherwise choose a time and place that is convenient to both of you.
4 Address the person directly as 'you'.
5 Give positive recognition to the person about who she or he is and what she or he does.
6 Reassure the person that the feedback is about her or his behaviour, in other words behaviours which she or he can choose to change.
7 Describe the specific non-assertive behaviour of the person.
8 Tell the person what you think or feel, know or imagine, using 'I' statements.
9 Listen to what the person says and how she or he expresses it carefully.

10 Remember that the person may feel threatened by your feedback and therefore behave non-assertively towards you.

11 Invite the person to ask questions for further clarification.

12 Encourage the person to give you feedback on how your behaviour influences her or his behaviour.

13 Be prepared to discuss with the person ways in which she or he can develop self-confidence and assertive behaviour.

14 Respect the person's wish to go away and think about the feedback.

15 Suggest that the person check out the feedback with others' perception of her or his behaviour.

16 Remember that when you give feedback to someone it often says more about you than the person to whom you are giving it.

Giving feedback to someone who has a negative attitude and passive behaviour

The person who has a negative attitude and whose behaviour is passive needs good quality feedback from you about her or his behaviour. People who have a negative attitude and who behave passively tend to expect others to be critical of them and that other people are better than them.

Thus when you do give feedback to these people they may either have a tendency to agree with you, if the feedback is critical of their behaviour, or alternatively they may complain to you that they had no control over their actions. Either way the challenge to you is to give feedback which is both positive and supportive of them; and to encourage them to take responsibility for their actions. These people tend to see themselves in the wrong and therefore it is important to find things that they have done which are 'right'.

Giving feedback to someone who has a negative attitude and manipulative behaviour

The person who has a negative attitude and behaves manipulatively needs feedback from you which is about her or his behaviour, especially positive feedback. People who have a negative attitude and whose behaviour is manipulative tend to see themselves and others as negative all the time. Giving them small amounts of good quality positive feedback is initially a way of breaking through this destructive attitude and behaviour.

The person is likely to believe the feedback if it is negative rather than if it is positive, tending to view positive feedback as untrustworthy. It is often difficult to find something positive to feedback to people who are so negative and whose behaviour is manipulative. Very often they are discounted and ignored by people, which serves to confirm their negative attitude towards themselves and others.

Whilst it is necessary to give others feedback which is critical of their behaviour so that they can develop and learn from it, people who have this destructive attitude and behaviour need a lot of specific positive and affirmative feedback before they can begin to be receptive to developing a positive attitude and assertive behaviour.

Giving feedback to someone who has a negative attitude and aggressive behaviour

The person who has a negative attitude and behaves aggressively also expects to receive negative and critical feedback about her or his behaviour. Often people who are aggressive try to defend themselves by giving feedback to others in an attempt to ward off any criticisms from them.

Generally speaking, they are unreceptive to feedback and do not seek it from others. Indeed you may tend to avoid giving them feedback for fear of their aggressive and defensive behaviour. Do remember that underneath this often angry and defensive behaviour is someone who has a low opinion of herself or himself, and who can only cope with this negative attitude by behaving aggressively towards others.

The more specific your feedback to the person the more receptive she or he will be to your feedback. She or he may shrug off positive feedback when you give it to her or him; however, over time you will find that the person will develop a more positive attitude towards themselves and others. The important thing is to keep giving them positive feedback and not to be put off by their aggressive and defensive behaviour.

RECEIVING GOOD QUALITY FEEDBACK

As a manager, receiving feedback from people is essential in order for you to manage effectively. Being open to and asking for feedback from the people with whom you work encourages them to talk about problems, and solutions, as they go along. Developing assertiveness in others involves not only giving good quality feedback but also being receptive and responsive to others and their feedback to you. People who give and receive good quality feedback are able to trust one another, and know where they stand with one another.

Frequently managers talk about having an 'open door' policy, suggesting that they are indeed open to receiving feedback from their colleagues. Whilst the door may be open they themselves are often closed to the feedback.

There is a tendency to defend and/or protect ourselves from feedback. All too often we anticipate criticism both of who we are and what we have done when someone tells us that they would like to give us some feedback. In other words we prepare ourselves for the worst rather than the best outcome, which results in a negative attitude and non-assertive behaviour. Typically people respond in such situations by behaving aggressively and strongly defending themselves or by behaving passively and protecting themselves.

The challenge then is to develop and maintain assertiveness in others, and in yourself, by being open and receptive to feedback. The following checklist on receiving feedback applies not only to developing assertiveness in others and maintaining assertive relationships but also in any situation in which you are receiving feedback.

Checklist: Receiving good quality feedback

1 Check that you have a positive attitude and that your behaviour is assertive.
2 Listen attentively to what the person is saying.
3 If you are unclear as to what the person is saying ask for clarification in the form of specific, behavioural examples. For example, 'Can you tell me exactly what you saw me doing when ...'.
4 Ask for time to think about the feedback.
5 If you are unsure as to whether the feedback is useful to you check it out with others. For example, 'When I chaired the meeting how did you see me behaving towards ...'.
6 Thank the person for her or his feedback.

Receiving good quality feedback from someone who has a negative attitude and passive behaviour

The person who has a negative attitude and whose behaviour is passive is unlikely to give you good quality feedback. People who have a negative attitude and behave passively assume that their view about things is irrelevant. They assume that what other people have to say is more important and better than anything they could contribute.

In order to receive good quality feedback from people whose behaviour is passive you will need to reassure them that you value and appreciate their views. Encourage them to be specific rather than to generalize. Reassure them that if they require further clarification on a subject under discussion they will be facilitating everyone's understanding of the subject. Make sure that you give them time to give their feedback and actively seek clarification from them.

Receiving good quality feedback from someone who has a negative attitude and manipulative behaviour

The person who has a negative attitude and whose behaviour is manipulative has a tendency to generalize and to always view things from a negative standpoint. The challenge to you is to encourage them to be more specific and to give feedback at the time rather than a long time after an event.

People whose behaviour is manipulative all too often give feedback a long time after an event and out of context. In this way they tend to mix the 'facts' with 'fantasy', presenting the feedback in a way which is difficult to relate to. Indeed you may have no recall of the event about which they are giving feedback and this makes it difficult to respond assertively to them. On such occasions it is useful to ask the person what has triggered off the giving of the feedback to you now, so long after the actual event. For example, a recent, and similar situation may have caused the person to decide to give feedback. If the person talks about other people and what she or he imagines they were thinking and/or feeling at the time tell her or him that you would rather hear about her or his experience.

The person needs to know that you do value feedback from her or him, and that you prefer feedback given as close to the event as possible. Also encourage the person to feedback to you her or his experience of the situation rather than what she or he thought others felt.

Receiving good quality feedback from someone who has a negative attitude and aggressive behaviour

The person who has a negative attitude and aggressive behaviour needs encouragement from you that feedback can be positive and that we all can learn from feedback, especially good quality feedback. People who behave aggressively tend to give feedback only when something goes wrong, and then they blame others for the mistake. They often think that if only they had done the job themselves it would have been done right.

In order to receive good quality feedback from them you will have to encourage them that you and others appreciate feedback which is about what has been done well and successfully, as well as feedback from which you can all learn so as to be successful next time.

Remember that people who have a negative attitude and behave aggressively tend to give themselves poor quality feedback and to focus on the negative aspects of their own behaviour. Thus the best way to receive good quality feedback from them is to help them to focus on the positive not only in themselves but also in others. Once they begin to be 'kinder' to themselves they will be able not only to be receptive to good quality feedback but also to give it to you and others.

REGULAR REVIEWING

The giving and receiving of feedback on a regular basis is the key to developing assertiveness in others and to developing and maintaining assertive working relationships. Regular reviewing involves using the communication skills described in Step Eight. It is about discussing openly both how the person is getting on in terms of developing assertiveness and how you and the person are developing an assertive working relationship. In other words, one in which you are both able to give to and receive from each other good quality feedback.

BENEFITS TO YOU, THE OTHER PERSON AND YOUR WORKING RELATIONSHIP

A person who feels respected by you will be far more receptive to your feedback and indeed may ask you for feedback in order to develop more assertive behaviour. You will enjoy a much more assertive and creative relationship with someone from whom you receive and to whom you give feedback.

CASE STUDY

In the following case study Allison is manager of the Buying Department (UK) for a large international retail company. She has had several years' experience in other retail companies and held a variety of posts, including managerial, within Buying and Marketing. She had held her current post for a period of about six months when she realized that, whilst her efforts to develop the team were succeeding, she was failing to communicate with one of the senior buyers.

Her relationship with Rosalind, the senior buyer, had been sensitive from the outset. Rosalind had applied for the post of manager and she, as well as many of her colleagues, had expected that she would get the job. She was an extremely successful buyer who enjoyed her work enormously. When it came to presenting her concepts to the Board of Directors she did so with confidence and a flair that was much envied by her colleagues.

At the time of Allison's appointment the company was undergoing a massive transition involving several forms of restructuring. Allison had been selected for the post of manager since she had experience not only of buying and marketing but also of managing.

Identifying the person's non-assertive attitude and behaviour

Allison knew that Rosalind had applied for the post she now held and she was not surprised that her relationship with her was difficult. At meetings Allison noticed that Rosalind avoided eye contact with her and that she often talked to a neighbour when she was addressing the team. When issues related to the reorganization were being discussed Rosalind either refused to comment or argued that Allison did not really understand the ways in which the team or the company worked. Allison found herself wanting to defend herself and argue back but knew that this would get neither of them anywhere.

She recognized herself in Rosalind in as much as whenever she felt threatened or pressured her own behaviour tended to be aggressive. She suspected that Rosalind's underlying Life Position was *I'm not OK – You're OK* but that her behaviour was also aggressive and her Life Position was *I'm OK – You're not OK*. She imagined that Rosalind had learnt to cope with her underlying lack of self-confidence by developing a fairly hard exterior which also gave her an apparent air of self-confidence.

Strategy: Giving good quality feedback

Allison decided that, given the difficult relationship between herself and Rosalind, the best strategy for helping Rosalind to develop her self-confidence and assertive behaviour would be to give her feedback on her behaviour. Initially she set about looking for opportunities to give Rosalind positive feedback. This meant, for example, acknowledging Rosalind's contributions at meetings. This was difficult for her to do since most of Rosalind's arguments were aimed at undermining her own suggestions; and because her instinct was to respond to Rosalind from an *I'm OK – You're not OK* Life Position. What made it easier for her was that she genuinely liked Rosalind and wanted to help her develop her self-confidence and assertive behaviour.

After several meetings at which Allison had acknowledged Rosalind's arguments and a presentation after which she had given her some positive feedback, Allison perceived Rosalind as being more relaxed in her presence. Nevertheless she observed that Rosalind continued to behave aggressively and defensively when any changes were being discussed as to working methods and procedures. Also she noticed that Rosalind was less enthusiastic about her work and that she lacked some of the old flair when making presentations.

She suggested to Rosalind that they arrange a convenient time for them to talk about her work and to talk about their working relationship. At first Rosalind replied by saying there was nothing to talk about as far as she was concerned. However, Allison said that she would welcome the opportunity to talk on a one-to-one now rather than to wait until Rosalind's appraisal which wasn't due for another three months. Reluctantly Rosalind agreed to a meeting and to thinking about her work in relation to the new procedures and restructuring; and her working relationship with Allison.

At this meeting Allison gave Rosalind positive feedback on her work and also feedback which was critical of her behaviour. She emphasized the importance to her of an assertive working relationship with her. Rosalind said that she felt more comfortable and relaxed with Allison in recent weeks but that since not getting the job as manager she had lost interest in her work. She didn't know if this was due to not getting the job or whether it was due to the current changes in the structure of the organization and the new procedures. She said that she felt more nervous prior to presentations to the board and less confident in herself.

Allison asked Rosalind what kind of support and encouragement she would like from her. Rosalind didn't really know what support she either wanted or needed since she prided herself in being able to manage without help from others; in fact she couldn't remember the last time she'd asked for support or help from anyone, let alone her boss. Allison suggested that she go away and think about what she wanted from her work for herself and what kind of support she needed in order to develop her self-confidence.

Regular reviewing

Rosalind did go away and think about herself, her work and her working relationship with Allison. Rosalind told me afterwards that she realized her whole identity – 'who she was' – was invested in her work; so long as it was going well she felt sufficiently confident in herself to perform well. However, when she failed to get the much wanted promotion she had nothing to fall back on in herself nor had she any friends or colleagues to whom she could turn for support. She felt extremely jealous of Allison, who she perceived as being much better suited for the job as manager but towards whom she harboured great resentment. On top of which she had not worked for a woman boss before and was finding this difficult.

Rosalind arranged to talk further with Allison and agreed with her that what she needed was much more positive feedback not only from Allison but also from the rest of the team. She imagined that the rest of the team perceived her as someone who didn't need positive feedback since she had masked her underlying lack of self-confidence by always appearing super confident. She also recognized that she didn't give positive feedback to her colleagues, who she tended to perceive not as colleagues but as competitors. She agreed not only to give more positive feedback to her colleagues but also to ask them for feedback. At the end of their discussion Allison told Rosalind that she enjoyed her company and that she looked forward to their continuing working relationship.

Rosalind reported afterwards that she hadn't realized just how difficult it was for her to receive positive feedback about herself, let alone about her work. She recognized that by maintaining an *I'm OK – You're not OK* Life Position she had managed to keep a distance between herself and others. It wasn't until Allison gave her feedback about her behaviour that she began to understand just how aggressive her behaviour had been towards others. Indeed she said that she was as critical with herself as she was towards others, especially her colleagues.

Benefits to Allison, Rosalind and their working relationship

After several months Rosalind noted that her attitude towards herself and others was much more positive; and although on occasions she found herself behaving aggressively towards others she was quickly able to change her behaviour thanks to the ongoing feedback from Allison and her colleagues. Their working relationship continued to be open and honest and one in which they both felt able to freely give and receive feedback from one another.

EXERCISE: DEVELOPING AND MAINTAINING ASSERTIVENESS IN OTHERS THROUGH GIVING AND RECEIVING GOOD QUALITY FEEDBACK

1   Select a person whose attitude is negative and behaviour non-assertive. The person may be someone with whom you would like to develop a more assertive and creative working relationship. She or he may behave assertively some of the time but for the most part when relating to you the person behaves non-assertively. If you have used your own positive attitude and assertive behaviour to influence the person and found that this has not helped her or him develop assertiveness, then giving good quality

feedback and opening up the working relationship through giving and receiving feedback is probably the next step. What is the person's negative attitude and non-assertive, or combination of non-assertive behaviours?
    Passive
    Manipulative
    Aggressive

2   Think of a recent and/or recurring situation in which you experienced the person as having a negative attitude and non-assertive behaviour. Imagine yourself entering the situation with a positive attitude and behaving assertively, and giving the person some good quality feedback about her or his behaviour. Remember to begin by giving the person some positive recognition which will help her or him to be more open and receptive to your feedback. Ensure that your feedback is specific and about the person's behaviour.
    Give specific examples of the feedback you would like to give the person.

3   What will the person be doing differently as a result of developing a positive attitude and assertive behaviour? Be specific so that the person knows exactly what having a positive attitude and behaving assertively means.

4   Regular reviewing. Be clear as to how often you and the person need to review the person's development. Find out what the person would like from you in terms of ongoing feedback and encouragement. Also be clear as to what you would like from the person in order to do your job more effectively and efficiently.

MY KEY ACTION

In order to develop and maintain assertiveness in others
through giving and receiving positive feedback, I need to:

THE NEXT STEP

The third strategy for developing and maintaining assertiveness in
others is counselling. Counselling is particularly useful when
people have not responded to you using your own positive attitude
and assertive behaviour to influence them, nor have they
responded to you giving good quality feedback to them. The
person for whom the counselling strategy is appropriate is usually
someone who has very low self-esteem. She or he is likely to have
a negative attitude and to behave non-assertively most of the time.

Step Eleven
Developing and maintaining assertiveness in others through counselling

In this section you have an opportunity to look at the ways in which:

- counselling can help people to develop and maintain assertiveness;
- you can counsel someone with whom you work in order to help her or him develop and maintain assertiveness.

A person who lacks self-confidence and whose behaviour is non-assertive is more likely to experience difficulties in relating to others and in her or his work. The person's lack of confidence can have a negative and potentially destructive influence not only on herself or himself but also on others. Initially, for example, you may have given feedback to the person and encouraged her or him to develop self-confidence and assertive behaviour. If, however, there has been no apparent development or change towards assertive behaviour you may decide that the person would benefit from counselling or alternatively a training course focusing on developing self-confidence and assertiveness.

It is unlikely that the person who is lacking in self-confidence will specifically ask you for help in the form of counselling. Indeed asking for help of any kind is often difficult for someone who is lacking in self-confidence and whose behaviour is non-assertive. Many managers decide to offer counselling to someone whose behaviour is such that it is having a negative impact on others as well as on the person herself or himself. Counselling someone whose Life Position is *I'm not OK – You're OK* or *I'm OK – You're not OK* is easier than counselling someone whose Life Position is *I'm not OK – You're not OK*, since the latter person is more likely to be depressed and unwilling to accept help from anyone unless challenged to do so, for example by the threat of losing her or his job.

You may decide that, because of your relationship with the person, you are not the best person to counsel her or him; or that the person requires a professional counsellor. Some companies do have in-house counsellors; sometimes the person prefers to be referred to a counsellor outside of the company.

If your relationship is such that you and the person are comfortable with the counselling relationship then you may find the counselling process described below a useful resource.

THE COUNSELLING PROCESS

1   Establishing the counselling relationship.
2   Helping the person to understand her or his non-assertive behaviour.
3   Helping the person explore and clarify ways of developing self-confidence and assertive behaviour.
4   Helping the person to commit to changing her or his behaviour from non-assertive to assertive.

1 Establishing the counselling relationship

It will help you in your role as counsellor if there is mutual trust and respect between you and the person. This is facilitated by:

■ selecting an environment which is conducive to counselling; private and free of any interruptions and one in which you are both likely to feel as comfortable and relaxed as possible.
■ being genuine, open and honest with the person. This includes being clear about (a) time and (b) confidentiality.

(a) Time

It is important to establish at the outset how much time you and the person have for the counselling. It is far better to let the person know at the outset that you have an hour than to run over the hour and be anxious about a meeting that you are missing. Likewise it is important that you encourage the person at the beginning to be assertive and to manage her or his time.

On occasions some managers have disagreed with me as to

whether counselling should be timed as such. My own experience of counselling individuals within organizations is that by being clear about the amount of time you and the person have available and/or are committed to helps establish the boundaries of the counselling relationship. Time constraints are part of organizational life. Managing your time and helping the person to manage her or his time effectively is part of developing self-confidence and behaving assertively.

(b) Confidentiality
Being genuine, open and honest may also involve reassuring the person of confidentiality if indeed you are able to offer confidentiality.

The issue of confidentiality is one which needs to be sorted out at the beginning of the counselling. Some managers, having agreed on confidentiality with the person, experience conflict when the person discloses something about herself or himself, or the situation, that they think others 'need to know'. Should this occur in your counselling it is important to ask yourself why you think others need to know. If, after careful consideration, you think it is necessary for someone else to know then encourage the person to tell them rather than yourself. If, however, the person is unwilling to do so then it is important that you respect her or his wishes. On the other hand the person may ask you to talk on her or his behalf, lacking the confidence at present to do so herself or himself.

The skills that you will need in order to establish the counselling relationship
The communication skills that were described in *Step Eight: Developing assertiveness through using the appropriate communication skills* will be enormously useful to you when you counsel someone. At this initial stage of the counselling process the following verbal and non-verbal communication skills will be useful in helping to develop trust and openness:

1   Talking the same language: listen carefully to the language that the person uses to talk about her or his experience. Does the person process information through a visual, auditory or kinesthetic sense-making process? Refer to the checklists of sense-making processes (pp. 92–3). Match the person's primary sense-making process.

2   Maintain eye contact, without staring at the person.
3   Reflect the person's body posture and then encourage her or him to relax by using your own relaxed breathing and open body posture. The person will at some point reflect your body posture and you can influence her or him to relax by being relaxed yourself. Refer to *Step Six: Developing assertiveness through relaxation*, in particular the breathing relaxation exercise (p. 70–1).

2 Helping the person to understand her or his non-assertive behaviour

The objective of the counselling is to help the person to develop her or his self-confidence and assertive behaviour. This is done by helping the person to talk about herself or himself and by helping her or him to understand how an underlying lack of self-confidence leads to non-assertive behaviour, be it passive, manipulative and/or aggressive behaviour.

The skills that you will need to help the person understand her or his lack of self-confidence, negative attitude and non-assertive behaviour

You will help the person to talk about herself or himself by asking open questions; open questions are those which begin with 'What ...', 'How ...', 'Which ...', 'When ...', 'Who ...' and 'Why ...'.

3 Helping the person to explore and clarify ways of developing self-confidence and assertive behaviour

Once the person understands her or his non-assertive behaviour and realizes that she or he can change it, you can help her or him to look at ways in which self-confidence can be developed.

Helping the person to explore a particular situation in which she or he lacked self-confidence and behaved non-assertively is a useful way of looking at what she or he could have done differently and the self-assertion skills she or he needs to practise. If the situation is one in which you were involved then you can give some specific feedback about the person's behaviour.

The skills that you will need to help the person explore and clarify her or his underlying lack of self-confidence, negative attitude and non-assertive behaviour

You will need to use the skills described above in the first two stages of the counselling process as well as the following skills:

1   Confronting: for example, if the person is saying one thing and doing something completely different. This might be an incongruency between what the person is saying and how she or he is expressing it in the counselling session. Alternatively, it might be a discrepancy between what the person has already told you earlier in the session and what they go on to say to you.

2   The skills of good quality feedback: you may have occasion to give the person some feedback on her or his behaviour and it will be especially important in the counselling session that it is good quality. Refer to the checklist 'Giving good quality feedback' (pp. 112–13).

3   Clarifying skills: when you are unclear as to what the person is saying reflect back to her or him what you think you have understood. This gives the person an opportunity to agree that this is exactly what she or he said or to disagree and to clarify for you and herself or himself any confusions.

4 Helping the person to commit to changing her or his behaviour from non-assertive to assertive

Most of us have mixed feelings about changing our behaviour, especially when it involves changing our underlying attitude from negative to positive. Initially it may seem extremely difficult for the person to imagine herself or himself thinking and feeling positive about self and others, and behaving assertively. Indeed helping someone to imagine the positive outcomes of behaving assertively is for many people the first step towards a change of attitude. Knowing that they can change their negative attitude and behaviour is in itself an affirmation of themselves.

At this stage in the counselling the person needs support and encouragement from you that she or he can change. It is important that you give positive recognition not only in support of the person's commitment to change but also when you observe her or him behaving differently after the counselling.

The skills of helping the person to commit to changing her or his behaviour from non-assertive to assertive
You will need action planning skills at this stage of the counselling process. In particular, you need to help the person set clear objectives; a mnemonic which I find useful is SMART. This stands for:

- **S**pecific
- **M**easurable
- **A**chievable
- **R**ealistic
- **T**ime oriented

Specific
In the role of counsellor you will need to help the person set objectives which are specific and not general. An objective which is specific is much more achievable than one which is vague and general. For example, the person may agree that she or he wants to develop and maintain a positive attitude and assertive behaviour. Once she or he is committed to this course of action you need to ask what will the person be doing differently as a result of having a positive attitude and behaving assertively.

Measurable
An objective which is specific is one which can be measured. In other words you and the person will be able to measure the changes she or he is making. You may agree to give the person feedback on what you observe her or him doing differently, for example, at the next meeting you both attend.

Achievable
It is important that the person who is developing assertiveness sets objectives that are achievable and therefore are motivating. Objectives which are unachievable have the opposite effect, they are demotivating and can lead to a further loss of self-esteem.

Realistic
Linked to the objectives being achievable is that of them being realistic. Objectives which are realistic have meaning for the person. The person feels that she or he will benefit from achieving the objectives and recognizes the value to her or him of developing

in real terms. For example, that she or he will have more energy, be more creative and productive.

Time oriented

The person needs to set objectives which are time oriented. Indeed in your role as counsellor it is important that you encourage the person to take small steps at first towards developing and maintaining assertiveness. Also to remind the person that having a positive attitude does not mean that she or he will behave assertively all the time. However, it does mean that she or he will be more readily aware of when her or his behaviour is non-assertive and of the assertive option.

COUNSELLING SOMEONE WHO HAS A NEGATIVE ATTITUDE AND WHOSE BEHAVIOUR IS PASSIVE

The goal of counselling people who have a negative attitude and whose behaviour is passive is to help them understand their negative attitude underlying their passive behaviour; and then to help them develop and maintain a positive attitude and assertive behaviour. People who behave passively tend to think that they have no control over what happens to them, they are victims. One of the first things that counselling can help them to realize is that they do have some control over what happens to them.

Once they recognize that they are responsible for much of what happens to them in their lives you can encourage them to look at things from a more positive and active perspective rather than passively sitting around letting things happen to them.

As they develop self-confidence and assertiveness they will be more willing to take on responsibility and to take risks, rather than shirking from responsibility and 'playing it safe'. It is important to reassure people that developing and maintaining self-confidence and assertiveness is about recognizing when they are behaving passively so that they can choose their behaviour. Being aware that they have a choice is probably the most significant aspect of developing and maintaining assertiveness for people whose attitude is negative and behaviour passive.

COUNSELLING SOMEONE WHO HAS A NEGATIVE ATTITUDE AND WHOSE BEHAVIOUR IS MANIPULATIVE

The goal of counselling people who have a negative attitude and behave manipulatively is to help them understand their underlying negative attitude and their manipulative behaviour; all too often people who behave manipulatively are unable to imagine behaving assertively. Their view of themselves and others is so negative that it is difficult for them to consider alternative ways of behaving. Your role as counsellor will probably be one of helping them to look at alternatives and in particular to consider looking at themselves and others from a positive perspective.

People who have a negative attitude and behave manipulatively frequently lie to themselves and others; however, their difficulty is that they believe their lies and/or believe that behaving manipulatively is the only way to behave. They imagine that everyone else is behaving manipulatively and that most people are to be mistrusted. Helping the person to trust herself or himself is often one of the ways of developing and maintaining a more positive attitude and assertive behaviour.

COUNSELLING SOMEONE WHO HAS A NEGATIVE ATTITUDE AND WHOSE BEHAVIOUR IS AGGRESSIVE

The goal of counselling people who have a negative attitude and whose behaviour is aggressive is to help them understand their underlying negative attitude, particularly towards others and their aggressive behaviour. Very often the person whose behaviour is aggressive thinks that it is the only way to behave and may have difficulty differentiating between what is aggressive and what is assertive behaviour.

A step towards helping people to develop and maintain assertiveness is often to help them understand that they are not in competition with everybody, and that they do not need to win over other people in order to respect themselves. Indeed very often the person who has to win over others walks away from the situation feeling awkward and uncomfortable about her or his behaviour.

Once the person has realized that she or he is behaving aggressively and defensively towards others in order to protect herself or himself, she or he can begin to develop and maintain self-confidence and assertive behaviours. Again this first step of recognition, that she or he has a choice of behaviour, is the beginning of developing and maintaining a positive attitude towards self and others, and assertiveness.

CASE STUDY

In the following case study Dave is the finance director for a computer company. He and his team work closely with the sales director and the sales team. He was not unduly surprised when his colleague, the sales director, gave him some feedback about the lack, and poor quality, of information that the sales team were getting from the finance team. He already knew that he had a problem with one of his finance managers, Martin, whose role it was to supply the sales director and team with financial accounting, reporting and business consultancy.

Earlier in the year Dave had reorganized the department and hoped that by doing so Martin's performance would improve. Unfortunately this had not happened and Dave had avoided dealing with the problem. He was angry with himself for having allowed the problem to grow to the point at which the sales director was now, justifiably, complaining about the lack of financial support from the finance team.

Recently the two teams had been on a management development course which had focused on personal and interpersonal awareness. The teams had been encouraged to look at themselves and the ways in which they could improve their working relationships as well as their working methods.

Identifying the person's non-assertive attitude and behaviour

Dave was aware that Martin had difficulties in relating not only to members of the sales team but also to members of his own finance team. The role of financial manager involves liaising with both teams in order to collect and communicate accurate information. Martin appeared to be more concerned with providing people with what he imagined they wanted to hear from him, rather than finding out what they actually needed by way of information. As a consequence he frequently blamed members of his own team when discussing issues with the sales team and all too often lied to members of both teams. This had led to confusion and misunderstandings between the two teams and to a blaming of one another when things were not working out.

On the management development course Martin had been called a liar by one of his own team. This had outraged Martin who, maintained that he valued his integrity more than anything else. He had returned from the course saying that the whole thing was a waste of time – unlike his colleagues all of whom had benefited greatly from the course whilst not always enjoying it.

Dave perceived Martin's behaviour as being manipulative. He appeared to lack the confidence to be straight with people, and would often play one person off another. In this way his behaviour was divisive and undermined the confidence of both teams. He diagnosed Martin's Life position as *I'm not OK – You're not OK.*

Selecting a strategy

Dave decided, as a result of the feedback from his colleague, that it was time for him to do more than give Martin feedback. On previous occasions when he had given Martin feedback on his behaviour Martin had strongly denied that he was supplying members of both teams with inaccurate information. Dave decided that he would talk to Martin about the course and ask him why he had found it to be such a waste of time.

He realized that he needed to help Martin develop and maintain self-confidence and assertive behaviour and that this would require careful counselling – probably over a period of time. He anticipated that Martin might initially be unreceptive to the counselling and that it would take time to develop trust between them. He also recognized that it would be important for him to maintain an *I'm OK – You're OK* Life Position and a positive attitude of mind. He knew that he would find this difficult to do sometimes since, like other members of the team, he was mistrustful of Martin. He imagined that Martin, likewise, was probably mistrustful of him.

At their first meeting Dave began by reassuring Martin of confidentiality. He told Martin that he was concerned about his performance, particularly since he had had complaints from the sales director about the information which they were receiving from the finance team in Martin's area of responsibility. He stated clearly that he wanted to discuss Martin's experience of the management development programme with him, and that he was aware that Martin had found it a difficult course. He said that his main concern was to help Martin develop and maintain his self-confidence and assertive behaviours which would help him relate openly and honestly with members of his own and the sales team.

At the end of this initial meeting Martin agreed that he needed help. He had disclosed to Dave that he felt depressed most of the time and that he found it difficult to relate to people since he didn't trust them or their motives. Indeed he said he found it difficult to talk to Dave for that very reason. He spent most of the time trying to work out what Dave was really after and imagining that he wanted to get rid of him. This resulted in him lying about himself and others partly, he said, because he felt he had nothing to lose by doing so.

Regular reviewing

Dave offered to talk with him on a weekly basis for the next couple of months. The purpose of the meetings, they agreed, would be to look at ways in which Martin could begin to trust and be more honest with himself, and as a consequence be more assertive with others. In particular Martin wanted others to respect him and his integrity. As a result of the course he had realized that others did not respect him nor did they see him as having integrity. It was the fact that others perceived him so very differently from how he wanted to be perceived which motivated him to accept the help that was being offered by Dave in the form of ongoing counselling.

Benefits to Dave, Martin and their working relationship

Martin realized that lying to his colleagues was having the opposite effect to the one which he desired, which was to please other people. Once he stopped trying to work out what he thought people wanted him to say and started to be direct and honest with them they started to seek him out and ask him for information. It was a slow process since he and they found it difficult to trust each other. However, the ongoing counselling session with Dave and the regular feedback from him helped Martin establish credibility with his own team and the sales team. Over time the quality of the information which he supplied to the sales team improved dramatically and the sales director felt that he could rely on Martin for accurate and relevant information.

EXERCISE: DEVELOPING AND MAINTAINING ASSERTIVENESS IN OTHERS THROUGH COUNSELLING

1 Select a person who you think would benefit from counselling in terms of helping her or him to develop and maintain a positive attitude and assertive behaviour. The person should be someone who you feel comfortable about offering counselling to, and who you feel would agree to your counselling her or him. The person is likely to be someone who you have already been helping to develop and maintain assertiveness through influencing and giving good quality feedback.

What is the person's negative attitude and non-assertive behaviour and/or combination of non-assertive behaviours?
Passive
Manipulative
Aggressive

2 Prepare yourself for counselling the person by making some notes about the counselling process:

- the particular skills that you will need to use at each stage of the process

- what feedback, if any, that you can give to the person about her or his behaviour.

MY KEY ACTION

In order to develop and maintain assertiveness in others through counselling them, I need to:

SUMMARY

You have now looked at three ways of helping people to develop and maintain assertiveness, influencing using your own behaviour, giving and receiving good quality feedback and counselling. Whichever strategy and/or combination of strategies you choose the key to helping others develop and maintain assertiveness is having a positive attitude and behaving assertively towards people yourself. Developing and maintaining assertiveness in yourself is therefore an essential part of managing others effectively and assertively.